IN CELEBRATION OF THE BOOK
Literary New Mexico

The following people were involved in the production of this handcrafted volume.

Co-editors:

[signature]
Dwight A. Myers

[signature]
Carol A. Myers

[signature]
Designer & Printer: Jene Lyon

[signature]
Copy Editor: Jetta Carleton

[signature]
Marbled Endpapers by Pamela Smith

[signature]
Frontispiece, "The Rio Grande," by Dan Stouffer

[signature]
Handmade Interleaves by Kathy Gurwell

[signature]
Binding by Roswell Bookbinding: Michael Roswell

IN
CELEBRATION
OF THE BOOK
Literary New Mexico

DWIGHT and CAROL MYERS, Editors

The New Mexico Book League
The Lightning Tree
Co-publishers
Albuquerque and Santa Fe, New Mexico

ISBN: 0-89016-063-5

Library of Congress Catalog Card Number:
81-83224

Manufactured in the United States of America

The New Mexico Book League
The Lightning Tree—Jene Lyon, *Publisher*

Albuquerque and Santa Fe, New Mexico   *U. S. A.*

*Dedicated to the Librarians and
Booksellers of New Mexico
Then—and Now.*

TABLE OF CONTENTS

PART TWO

Seventy-seven courageous New Mexicans, listed in alphabetical order, reveal the three books that had the greatest impact on their lives.

George Agogino, Rudolfo A. Anaya, Phelps Anderson, Ruth Armstrong, Lura Bennett, Jeff Bingaman, Helen Blumenschein, Jeanne Bonnette, William J. Buchanan, Richard Buhler, Alice Bullock, Jetta Carleton, Marsie Cate, Fray Angélico Chávez, Peggy Pond Church, Saul Cohen, Roger B. Corbett, Frank J. Crosby.

Baba Ram Dass, William E. Davis, Edwin J. Delattre, Stephen R. Donaldson, Rosalie F. Doolittle, Don Dresp, Concha Encinias, Richard W. Etulain, George H. Ewing, G. Ward Fenley, Gene Frumkin, Tony Hillerman, Vida Hollis, Gary House, Genevieve Janssen, David Marcus Johnson, James Ralph Johnson, Teddy Keller, Bruce King.

Clifford E. Lange, Betty Lloyd, Manuel Lujan, Jr.,

Jene Lyon, John D. McKee, Thomas J. McLaughlin, James Mafchir, Edwin L. Mechem, Mark Medoff, Gen. Hugh Meglone Milton II, John Nichols, Thelma Nord, T. M. Pearce, Lynn Perrigo, James Powell, Lee Priestley, Harvena Richter, Jack D. Rittenhouse, John Donald Robb, David Rusk, Tom Rutherford.

Louis E. Saavedra, Polly Schaafsma, Harrison Schmitt, Paul Bigelow Sears, Marc Simmons, John L. Sinclair, Joe Skeen, Diana Stein, Joe Stein, Richard Martin Stern, Gerald W. Thomas, Justine Thomas, Clyde W. Tombaugh, David H. Townsend, Frederick Turner, Peter van Dresser, Frank Waters, Victor Westphall, Norman Zollinger.

FOREWORD

As a relocated Southern Californian in Southern Arizona, I might well have sought refuge in Northern New Mexico if there had been more abundant book resources to meet my needs. The friendly charm of two small bookshops—the Taos and Villagrá—I first knew 30 years ago; the beauty of landscape and a sense of history made it a region of great attraction.

Yet, grist for my mill lay in books and periodicals, documents and maps in massive numbers. For these the University of New Mexico library was my best source. Another excellent source was the State Library in Santa Fe. For what it does in general reference work and in supplying local libraries throughout New Mexico, the State Library has a proud record going back to Julia Brown Asplund, the visionary founder of New Mexico's model library extension service. While I was living in Santa Fe one summer and writing chapters that appeared in *Southwest Classics,* the State Library provided me with reference service, friendship and coffee.

New Mexico has never stopped calling, and I answer the call with trips or talk. Old friends have gone—Haniel Long and Erna Fergusson,

Bill Wallace, Clinton Anderson and Tom Popejoy, Frieda Lawrence and Claire Morrill in death; Paul Horgan to the eastern frontier, Roland Dickey to the western. New friendships have been formed with the likes of Jack Rittenhouse, Saul Cohen, Marc Simmons and Dwight Myers. In them I recognize the bookish spokesmen New Mexico needs if it is to reach bibliographic maturity to match its eminence in the arts and sciences.

To each generation a challenge. Julia Asplund and Erna Fergusson responded in their time and their way. Now with the stimulation and needling provided by the New Mexico Book League, the future looks more hopeful. If I were to wish for as much life again as I have been blessed with for 75 years, I would ask to be native to the Land of Enchantment and to answer the challenges of times to come. That books will be an indispensable part of the state's culture is my wish and my hope.

So here is a bow to the New Mexico Book League and all that they are doing to arouse the public conscience. May the power of many books be theirs.

Bajada of the   Lawrence Clark Powell
Santa Catalinas

INTRODUCTION

It is perhaps correctly assumed by historian Marc Simmons that the very first book "ever opened and read under New Mexico's shining turquoise sky" was brought north out of New Spain by the priest, Fray Marcos de Niza, in 1539. But if one questions this claim for Fray Marcos, then most certainly 1540 would be the honored first year for the appearance of a book in New Mexico as part of the carefully chosen baggage of the five friars who accompanied Coronado. The ownership of books stayed almost exclusively within the family of clerics for hundreds of years. The Franciscans found it quite troublesome when non-clerics read of matters which they were not prepared to discuss nor had the ability to defend. In "Books in New Mexico, 1598-1680," *New Mexico Historical Review,* July 1942, by Eleanor Adams and France Scholes, there is the famous quote of Fray Juan Bernal, Commissary of the Holy Office, who in 1669 wrote:

> I consider it an extremely undesirable thing that certain laymen of this kingdom should have in their houses *Summas de Theologia Moral,* because they do not understand what they read. . .or grasp the meaning as they should because of the manner in which the summarists express it by question and interrogatory, which these readers take for affirmation.

This attitude prevailed well into the 19th century as we hear of decree after decree commanding the various governors to find and destroy certain books that disseminated depraved writings which contained liberty slogans and advocated independence. But as Marc Simmons points out, this effort was "more ludicrous than sinister;" the simple folk of New Mexico were, for the most part, neither readers nor writers.

The history of the book in New Mexico is dominated heavily by printing presses and volumes determined to be of value to the Church. This control of books limited to theological interests began to break down about 1880.

Most certainly the first "bookstores" in the territory were in the shops in mission churches. We know that these stores sold the prime necessities until an entrepreneur came on the scene, and most certainly these necessities included religious books. The first regular bookseller, according to Nancy May, was probably Walter V. Hayt of Santa Fe, who in the 1880 census listed his occupation as "Bookseller."

It would appear that Cobean's Book and Stationery Co. of Roswell is indeed the oldest store still in operation that has sold books continuously. On December 5, 1916, Cobean's paid Oxford University Press $5.41 for Bibles sold that Christmas. They also have records showing that they dealt with New York Book Co.

and other wholesalers and printers as early as 1916. This comes from a hand-posted ledger kept by Mary P. Cobean, aunt of the current proprietor, Ruth Cobean McPherson.

The oldest pure bookstore still in operation is the venerable Villagrá Book Shop in Santa Fe, which began in the early 1920s. Two of the most prominent bookstores New Mexico has ever had were the New Mexico Bookstore (later, New Mexico Book Co.) of Albuquerque and the Santa Fe Book and Stationery Co. Both date to the 1920s and discontinued operation about 1960. The stores still in existence after long histories show one common thread that has led to their continuing success—personal involvement and interest in their customers' lives. None was driven by get-rich-quick motives.

The history of our libraries parallels that of our bookstores except that it reaches further back. The first libraries, like the early shops, were housed in mission churches. The books, all religious, were most often personal possessions of the local priest. It was also in 1880 that libraries started to make inevitable changes. By 1900 Albuquerque claimed to have the largest and best free public library in the Southwest; one supported by a local tax. In 1887 an appropriation of $8,000 was given to the Territorial Library for the purchase of books. By 1900 this library, now the New Mexico State Library, contained 5,600 volumes plus a collection of law books.

By 1980 most New Mexico towns with a population of at least 1,000 had a public library. Many smaller towns enjoy some sort of organized collection of books for public lending, usually sponsored by a local women's club, a church, or, in some rare instances, by a local business. There are 40 organized public libraries and many private or institutional libraries which our general public may use. In 1974 the then 39 public libraries had 1,270,070 volumes, or 1.5 books per capita. In 1979-80 our 40 public libraries spent $3,544,506 on salaries, $1,011,156 on materials including books, and had a combined total of 1,584,986 books checked out by 454,114 card holders. But because of the growth of the state, we fell to but 1.2 books per capita. In 1981 the University of New Mexico library officially accessed its one-millionth volume.

The story of books in New Mexico is of course far more complicated than a recitation of facts and figures. The purpose of this book is to celebrate the tenth anniversary of the New Mexico Book League, an organization serving a multilingual populace. According to the 1980 U.S. Census, one of several Indian languages was the mother tongue of 8% of our citizens, Spanish the mother tongue of 36.6% of the people, and

English the mother tongue of most of the rest.

On May 10, 1971, I asked three Albuquerque bookpeople—Wayne Hammond, owner of Plaza Books, Inc.; A. O. Jackson, manager of U.N.M. Bookstore; and Manfred Carpenter, manager of Book World (the Beck News Agency retail store)—to join me for lunch at the Elks Club. The purpose of this meeting was to discuss the founding of a book association to serve the state. On May 13 Peggy Tozer of Eastern New Mexico University Library agreed to make a presentation to the New Mexico Library Association, of which she was President, to enlist their aid in this endeavor.

By October the first draft of our constitution, prepared by Wayne Hammond, was presented to an enlarged group including Jack Rittenhouse, Edward Holman, Sister Rita, Alan Clark and John Sigler. The final organizational meeting, held in November, included Dr. Kenneth Sollitt, Anne Nagel, Frank Skinner, Dr. Eleanor McCloskey, Martin and Marilyn Ruoss, William Farrington and Eleanor Pickett. And on February 25, 1972, we became an officially incorporated organization: The New Mexico Book League.

Our purpose was to bring together all people interested or involved in books "to enrich the cultural life in New Mexico through the popularization of reading." We sponsored a book review program for years on KOAT-TV, the ABC station in Albuquerque. We sponsored a two-page advertisement in *Publishers Weekly* to promote the small publishers in New Mexico, and we began publishing *Book Talk*, which continues to appear five times a year. Subscriptions have averaged around 400 a year. Our membership in 1980 lived in 44 New Mexico communities, 12 other states, and in Germany and Canada.

Whenever an author faces the task of marketing a manuscript, the Book League does everything possible to get the project properly placed. We have successfully aided publication of such books as *Riders to Cibola* by Norman Zollinger, *Indians of the American Southwest* by Dr. Bertha Dutton and *Skystone and Silver* by Carl Rosnek and Joseph Stacey.

When requested, our members give advice and counsel to anyone interested in starting a bookstore in the state. We involved ourselves in the White House Council on Libraries in Washington, D.C., in November 1979. And we shall continue to offer our services to any person whose interest is in the furtherance of books in New Mexico.

All contributors to this anniversary celebration volume have allowed us to use their efforts at no cost and we are indebted to each of them. We have striven for excellence in both content and production. As much as possible has been done by hand: the marbled endpapers and hand-made interleaves, the type entirely hand-set, the frontispiece specially commissioned for the book. In the writing, editing and production the project has been an effort of love by almost a hundred people. To borrow the words of Kurt Vonnegut, this book is "an experiment with composing music for the eye, resulting in a simple hymn for the printing press."

Dwight A. Myers
Executive Director,
New Mexico Book League

IN CELEBRATION OF THE BOOK
Literary New Mexico

PART ONE

A SORCERER'S APPRENTICE IN THE LAND OF ENCHANTMENT

Jack D. Rittenhouse

FEW STATE slogans are as apt as that of New Mexico: "The Land of Enchantment." Lilian Whiting was first to use it as a book title, in 1906, and she was writing about the entire Southwest. In 1935 or soon thereafter, New Mexico staked a claim to it when state tourist director Joe Bursey and publicist Ward Hicks began to use it.

Anyone who has lived in New Mexico knows that the region does cast a spell. The land itself enchants, but there are those sorcerers who can cast the magic across great distances, to lure newcomers as the sirens lured Ulysses. These are the writers and photographers and painters, and the printers and publishers who transport the witchery. They are sorcerers in print, and the editors, librarians, and booksellers are the sorcerers' apprentices.

These necromancers work insidiously and indirectly. They do not attempt to proselyte, they merely let the spell appear in words or pictures. They do not attempt to convert the undecided, partly because New Mexicans do not want the world to become houseguests. They do not debate the subject, because New Mexicans have learned that reactions to the region are seldom bland but are violently for or against this haunting, arid land. Defending one's choice of a place in which to live is like defending one's choice of a husband or wife. It is quite understandable to the couple but may be incomprehensible to others.

Nevertheless, each of us does try at times to explain this choice, to describe the spell of New Mexico. It may be an act of self-reassurance, to justify to ourselves why we forego a higher income we might earn elsewhere, or it may be an attempt to explain to friends back East why we have forsaken the metropolitan life.

A few years back, before I retired from the University of New Mexico Press as their editor of Western books, Tony Hillerman and I discussed this on campus. We particularly sought to understand the impact New Mexico has on the minds of those who come here. There does seem to be something about New Mexico that not only attracts creative people but stimulates their creativity. And this is no capsuled stimulant that can be strewn by travel publicists or land promoters. New Mexico's status as a haven for visual artists, the painters and photographers, has long been accepted. It is less well known

 4

that we are also home territory for novelists and poets.

Tony and I re-examined the writings of D. H. Lawrence, Mary Austin, Oliver La Farge, Conrad Richter, Winfield Townley Scott, Lawrence Clark Powell, and even the European psychiatrist C. G. Jung to see what impact New Mexico had on their minds. Dr. Marta Weigle pointed us to other writers who had described the effect New Mexico had on their mind and lifestyle.

Out of this came Tony Hillerman's book, *The Spell of New Mexico,* built around selected excerpts from those writers.

Conrad Richter wrote once that when he moved to New Mexico he found "more interesting people to the square kilometer than any place [he] had ever known." Jacquetta Hawkes, writing with J. B. Priestley in their *Journey Down a Rainbow,* said she found that Santa Fe had "twenty-five times as much creative energy per capita as any other city in the world."

Why should this be so?

Richter continued, in describing his move from Pennsylvania to New Mexico, "It was the most significant move we ever made. Not for anything would we have wanted to miss the incomparably rich experience of the Southwest. From the very first we grew aware of phenomena in sensation. Now love is a very strange and pow-

erful thing. It seems silly to suppose that such an inanimate object as a place or region can respond to this mysterious emotion and return it. And yet, curiously enough, that is exactly what came to pass."

D. H. Lawrence was similarly affected. He wrote in one of his essays, "Superficially the world has become small and known. Poor little globe of earth, the tourists trot around you as easily as they trot around the Bois or around Central Park. There is no mystery left; we've been there, we've seen it, we know all about it, we've done the globe, and the globe is done.

"This is quite true, superficially," Lawrence continued. "On the superficies, horizontally, we've been everywhere and done everything. Yet the more we know, superficially, the less we penetrate. As a matter of fact, our great-grandfathers, who never went anywhere, in actuality had more experience of the world than we have, who have seen everything. When they listened to a lecture with lantern-slides, they really held their breath before the unknown, as they sat in the village schoolroom. We, bowling along in a rickshaw in Ceylon, say to ourselves, 'It's very much what you'd expect.' We really know it all. We are mistaken. I realized this with shattering force when I [came] to New Mexico. I think New Mexico was the greatest experience from the outside world that I have ever had. It certainly changed me forever."

Mary Austin, in her *The Land of Journey's Ending,* approached the same idea from another side when she wrote, "There can be no adequate discussion of a country, any more than there can be of a woman, which leaves out the inexplicable effect produced by it on the people who live there. If more lines of natural development converged here, between the bracketing rivers, more streams of human energy came to rest than anywhere else within what is now the United States, it was because men felt here [in the Southwest] the nameless content of the creative spirit in the presence of its proper instrument. Such a country as this calls its own from the four world quarters."

And Oliver La Farge, in an article about the state, once wrote, "What is New Mexico? How sum it up? It is a vast, harsh, poverty-stricken, varied, and beautiful land, a breeder of artists and warriors. It is the home, by birth or by passionate adoption, of a wildly assorted population which has shown itself capable of achieving homogeneity without sacrificing its diversity. It is primitive, undeveloped, overused, new, raw, rich with tradition, old, and mellow. It is itself, an entity, a land that draws and holds men and women with ties that cannot be explained or submitted to reason."

7

The famed psychiatrist, C. G. Jung, once wrote of a visit he made to Taos Pueblo. "We always require an outside point to stand on, in order to apply the lever of criticism. Through my trips to and in America, I have obtained an enormous amount of insight into the European character. There [in Taos] for the first time I had the good fortune to talk with a non-European, that is, to a non-white. I was able to talk with him as I have rarely been able to talk with a European."

While Jung used New Mexico as a mirror to help him understand himself, the poet Winfield Townley Scott tried to understand what the land does to others. He wrote, in one of his few prose works, "What is there about this land which sets travelers to altering their schedules and overstaying? What is there, more forcefully still, that has seized upon astonishing numbers of people who came to look, and then set down their luggage and remained?" Scott also added that "May Sarton, the poet and novelist, put it well when she said, 'Here you can say you are a writer and they say "Fine!" They don't say, "Who's your agent? When's your next book coming out?"'"

Harvey Fergusson, in another essay, also commented on the newcomers. "The latest invasion of this much invaded land has been an influx of painters and writers and of all those various types of men and women who are the camp followers of every cultural movement. This westward movement of the men with paint and ink on their fingers has given New Mexico a new type of society and a new spurt of life, just as the coming of the beaver trappers and wagon traders did. In New Mexico the painters and writers seem to be more a part of the society they have invaded than anywhere else I have been. Here surely is a place where many kinds of men live and work, where one may dig or dream, make poems, bricks, or love, or merely sit in the sun, and find tolerance and some companionship. Here handicraft as well as the machine has some place in life, the primitive persists beside the civilized, the changeless mountains offer refuge to the weary sons of change.''

These perceptive writers made their point well, and if you need more you will find it in Hillerman's book, *The Spell of New Mexico.* That spell has carried far. Once on a trip to Vancouver, British Columbia, I naturally found time to stop in an antiquarian bookstore. There, hundreds of miles from New Mexico, I found on the shelf Irwin Blacker's novel, *Taos,* Frieda Lawrence's *Not I But the Wind,* also two books in Lars Lawrence's proletarian trilogy on New Mexico, and John Nichols' *The Milagro Beanfield War.* Above, on a high shelf, were two small books on the mines of New Mexico that

9

I had printed at my Stagecoach Press. And when I came back that evening and stopped at the U. S. border immigration and they asked for proof of citizenship, I showed them my New Mexico driver's license and my identification card from the University of New Mexico library. Both were accepted as proof enough.

Yet some would disagree mildly with Harvey Fergusson when he said that writers are the latest invasion. They were the *first* invaders, and the spreading of the spell began with the report of Alvar Nuñez Cabeza de Vaca written after his journey in this region in 1532-1536. If he probably never entered New Mexico itself he came close enough to it to entice Coronado north a few years later. And the accounts of Coronado's journey encouraged Don Juan de Oñate to march north and establish our first real colony. And with Oñate came Gaspar Pérez de Villagrá, Oñate's poet-historian, a true Renaissance gentleman in the combination of arms, courtesy, and letters, whose history in verse appeared in 1610, the first written on the North American continent.

Other Spaniards continued to come to New Mexico and write of what they saw: Gerónimo de Zarate Salmeron in 1626; Fray Alonso de Benavides in 1630 and 1634; Carlos de Sizuenza y Góngora, whose *Mercurio Volante* was printed in 1692; and Fray Francisco Atanasio Domínguez, who wrote of the missions of New Mexico in 1776.

Even into the nineteenth century the Spaniards were still writing about New Mexico. Don Pedro Bautista de Pino wrote a descriptive report on New Mexico in 1812, and Antonio Barreiro wrote another in 1832. And their heirs and descendants still help spread the spell of New Mexico: an entire clan of Espinosas, scholarly José, the lawyer-historian Gilberto, the folklorist Carmen, each concerned with a different view of New Mexico's past. The roster of others is long, from Fabiola Cabeza de Baca to Rudolfo Anaya.

Zebulon Pike spread the mystique of New Mexico when his report was published in 1810, luring Augustus Storrs and other Missourians to open the Santa Fe Trail in 1821. During the next few decades we had other sorcerers casting their runes: James Ohio Pattie, Josiah Gregg, George Ruxton, Lewis Garrard and Susan Magoffin. Each of these helped others perceive that perhaps here might be the land of their heart's desire.

This spell of New Mexico falls on many types of people. Some write no poems and paint no pictures but just enjoy living here, working in ordinary jobs. But the spell continues to bring writers, book designers, printers, publishers, booksellers and librarians—excellent people who often would be outstanding in the largest centers and at the highest salaries, but they chose New Mexico for their own satisfaction, and in return they enrich us all. They like the land and they like the people; they find kindred minds who speak the same language of heart and soul. And as they bring benefits to us they also enrich themselves from us in a chain reaction of creativity. There are, naturally, others who come here to manipulate, to promote themselves, or to make the quick gain, but sooner or later they find themselves uneasy, out of place, and they move on. We rarely miss them.

But those who stay find that the sight and color of the land creep inside them. Their audiences respond like the opposing prongs of a tuning fork, intensifying creativity. Their writing comes closer to the earth, nearer to reality, and artificiality drops away. The landscape overwhelms the artist, as do the faces of the people. A sense of past history and a vista of the future creep into every writer's theme and style. There are fewer status symbols because people do not need the symbols, they have the status. In every field of creative art, never underestimate a stranger in New Mexico: he or she may have a national reputation that here wears an unassuming exterior.

Many who live elsewhere and have felt the spell of New Mexico but cannot come here build collections of Southwestern books. In this part of the world, we had book collectors before we had printers or bookshops or public libraries. When Bishop Zumarraga arrived in Mexico City in 1528, he brought his own collection of two hundred books, the first private library in the New World. He was instrumental in bringing the first printing press to the continent, in 1539, and one of the books done on that press, the Spanish-Nahuatl dictionary for which the press was imported, is now in the special collections at the University of New Mexico.

When Don Diego de Vargas died at Bernalillo in 1704, he left his own collection of thirty-three books, listed by title in his effects. The wagons that rolled a century later over the Santa Fe Trail brought books, just as had the Mexican caravans that came up from Chihuahua.

Some of the great New Mexico collections have been given to university libraries within New Mexico. A few other fine collections have gone elsewhere, because we lacked the funds or the influence to keep them here: the papers of L. B. Prince, the William Ritch papers and those of Maurice Garland Fulton and Patrick Hurley.

Many of the finest collections of books about New Mexico are built by collectors who live here. The subject of the Southwest leads all

13

other topics as a field of collecting, but our collectors are not provincial. One man has a superb collection of Sherlock Holmes material; another has ten thousand items on the subject of the dance; down near Silver City two British ranchers built a fine collection of Dickens' works. A graduate student at one university had shelves filled with five thousand works on herpetology, and in Portales Jack Williamson built an outstanding science fiction collection. To list all of their names would be unwise, for we have itinerant thieves who regard such lists as treasure maps.

These collectors who specialize in books on the Southwest have not simply fallen under the spell of New Mexico, they have become completely bewitched and are therefore some of the happiest people one could meet.

Collectors, of course, can combine the thaumaturgy of New Mexico with the excitement of the chase, for they know that the rarest game is still afoot. Within the past year a copy of one of the earliest New Mexico books, a little forty-eight page pamphlet printed by Padre Martínez in Taos, was found by a book scout who sold it to a California dealer who in turn found a ready buyer in New Mexico willing to pay $2,300 for it. When the idea of acquiring a copy of Hakluyt's *Voyages* was advanced as a possibility for the millionth volume in the University

14

of New Mexico library, not a single great book-seller in this country or Europe had a copy for sale, yet one turned up when the library of a British castle was liquidated.

Libraries are relatively new in the South-west, except for those kept as private collections. In 1850 Congress appropriated the sum of five hundred dollars for the purchase of books for a territorial library in New Mexico. With the customary congressional confusion, they allotted only one hundred dollars a year for a librarian's salary. That post, therefore, was often vacant or staffed by an unqualified person, and in the next thirty years the library managed to gather only about 1,800 books.

But by 1860 the Territory of New Mexico did have fifteen public libraries and two church libraries, with combined holdings of about eleven thousand volumes. And in the past decades we have come to realize that there is a spell of New Mexico that applies to librarians as well as to anyone else, perhaps more so. Patricia Paylore, born in Roswell and later one of Arizona's great librarians, said twenty years ago, "A good librarian in the Southwest must have a feeling for the land. One has only to turn back to the land to find new faith and renewed strength. A good librarian must feel the pull and power of this dry and ancient land, because only in this way can he interpret it and understand its people

15

and their needs, as well as its social structure and his place in it."

She went on to say, "In the arid Southwest it takes more to be a good librarian than elsewhere. An ordinary man just won't do. There have been a lot of them. They come and go all over the Southwest and they leave no mark. For first of all they have no feeling for the land, and next they take and do not give, and finally they —will you forgive me for being crude?—they have no guts. Are there no more pioneers? Is the frontier really gone? And I challenge the library profession to breach it."

Miss Paylore's full talk was reprinted in No. 3 of the *Occasional Papers* of the UCLA library, and it should be required reading for every worker in every library in the Southwest.

There have been librarians who have left their mark on New Mexico, even since the Paylore gauntlet was thrown. Scholars and ordinary readers will remember Gertrude Hill and Ruth Rambo at the Museum of New Mexico library, and Katherine McMahon in the Southwest collection in the old building of the Albuquerque Public Library, as well as William S. Wallace at New Mexico Highlands University. These are only a few among those who have retired or moved on. Among others who will be unforgettable must certainly be Octavia Fellin, who made the Gallup Public Library so well-known locally that one Gallup firm's roadside billboard carries its address as being "across from the public library." Would that every library became such a Greenwich meridian! And if one started to evaluate the present public and university librarians, the list would be long.

These people did and are doing what J. Frank Dobie, a writer of Southwestern classics, asked be done when he wrote of the Southwest's landscape: "I am at home here, and I want to know more about my home land. I want to live intelligently on it. I want certain data that will enable me to accommodate myself to it. Knowledge helps sympathy to achieve harmony."

These librarians have also taken to heart Lawrence Clark Powell's statement that "We have cornered the region's books but not its wisdom." The essential function of a library is to bring the book and the reader together. Powell does this in every talk he makes, and in every article and book he writes. He is the great evangelist of the book, and we owe him an immeasurable debt.

But libraries and collectors would have no books were it not for the printers and publishers. In this sector the spell of New Mexico has brought a remarkable range of talent. Elsewhere in this book the story is told of the books published by Padre Martínez in 1834 and of other unusual printers and publishers down to the present.

17

There were others in the graphic arts, on a lesser scale, who left their mark on the land. At the start of the 1920s Spud Johnson used a little platen press in Taos to print his journal, *Laughing Horse,* one of the first of many personal presses in New Mexico. Another was the designer-publisher Edward McLean, who spent some time in New Mexico and Colorado and developed his skill. In 1947, over the imprint of Libros Escogidos at Washington, D. C., McLean published the first accurate translation of a New Mexico folk classic, *Vicente Silva and His Forty Bandits.* It was a superbly designed book.

The artist-designer Gustave Baumann was the region's great master of the wood-block print; some say the nation's best. Baumann came to New Mexico in 1918 and spent the rest of his life in Santa Fe creating wood-block prints in many colors, grinding his own pigments for inks and making limited runs on a small handpress. That printing press is now in the studio of Helen Gentry in Santa Fe. Helen, who was in New Mexico during the 1930s, has returned to the land whose spell could not be broken. She was first among America's women to be given a one-woman showing by the American Institute of Graphic Arts. In a San Francisco library there is a permanent collection of her full works, but she has yet to be given comparable recognition within the state she calls home.

 18

We have had others also. Thomas Benrimo is remembered as a printer for his colorful edition of Joseph O. Foster's poetic drama, *The Great Montezuma*, with each signature in a different color of ink. In 1940 Dorothy Stewart in Santa Fe had a platen press, The Pictograph Press, for which she handset and printed an abridged edition of *A Midsummer Night's Dream* and other works, including one on Indian dances illustrated with multicolor linoleum blocks.

Her friend Agnes Sims also issued a memorable work, *San Cristobal Petroglyphs*, at the Southwest Editions press in Santa Fe in 1950, although it was more portfolio than book. A superb silkscreen or serigraph artist, Louis Ewing, has created remarkable works in that technique. My own Stagecoach Press, active in Santa Fe from 1962 to 1967, when it was adjourned *sine die*, attempted to work in the fine-press tradition. Jon and Louise Webb operated their Loujon Press briefly in Santa Fe in the early 1960s, moving there from New Orleans. They moved on to Tucson but returned to Albuquerque, where the venture ceased. The Loujon books used a variety of papers and designs in each book, and the text emphasized poetry and the work of Henry Miller. The latest, and possibly the best to work in the fine-press tradition is Linnea Gentry's Amaranth Press, which was moved from California to Santa Fe late in 1980. Nearly all of these presses printed directly from type, using letterpress with much hand work.

The state has seen a continuing growth in individual publishers who spread the spell of New Mexico. Such firms as the Rio Grande Press, Calvin Horn, Sunstone Press and The Lightning Tree, are continuing the tradition of regional books that interpret the Southwest.

The largest publisher in the state is the University of New Mexico Press, which emphasizes both scholarly and regional works. For many years it was headed by Roland Dickey, a designer who was trained in New Mexico. The Museum of New Mexico Press has broadened its scope and advanced its quality in design.

Books move from these presses through the bookstores, and it is in this sector that we have seen the greatest mushrooming in recent years, so much so that one wonders if some mechanism has run wild in the incantation, as it did in the tale of the sorcerer's apprentice.

To paraphrase *The Rubaiyat,* one wonders what the bookdealers buy, one-half as precious as the books they sell. The 1905 state business directory listed sixteen book outlets in eleven towns, with three in Albuquerque, two each in Las Vegas, Socorro, and Tucumcari, with one in Santa Fe and in each of six other towns.

In the 1950s the most active shops in Albuquerque were Jim Threlkeld's in the downtown

 20

area and Emily Ramage's on Nob Hill. Nancy Lane had the Villagrá Bookshop in Santa Fe, Claire Morrill and Genevieve Janssen were at the Taos Book Shop, and Betty Armstrong was doing well at her Mesilla Bookshop. The principal shops handling only antiquarian books were the Tom Davies shop in Albuquerque and the Ancient City shop in Santa Fe. In Las Vegas La Galería de los Artesanos sold both old and new books. Today all of these except the Las Vegas shop have new owners.

The tidal wave of paperbacks that came after World War II put larger racks in drugstores, supermarkets and discount houses. New-book stores moved into the shopping centers and chain bookstores entered the scene. College bookstores enlarged and carried broader lines. The antiquarian bookshops increased in number and in quality.

But as the volume of bookselling increased, the proportion of regional books remained high. Whether in the section of shelves labeled "Southwestern" or scattered throughout every part of the shop, the bestselling books told people how to build, cook, travel, draw, grow, camp, decorate and collect in the New Mexico style.

This attempt to explain the spell of New Mexico by portraying its various sorcerers: authors, collectors, librarians, printers, publishers, and booksellers, might be illustrated better as a

21

web with many strands, all interlocked. At the center might be the New Mexico Book League, an organization whose members are from all the strands. Anyone not familiar with the League's publication, *Book Talk*, verges on regional illiteracy. The League's hard-driving executive director, Dwight Myers, is one of the chief wizards in promoting the spell of New Mexico.

These and all of the others, mentioned and not mentioned, are part of the group who not only spread the mystique of New Mexico but have themselves blatantly accepted that spell and have been shaped by it. As Mary Austin wrote, these people "knew what they wanted, and moved instinctively by the shortest cuts to a true Western accomplishment. The spell works so deeply that often the only notice of its perpetual activity is a profound content in the presence of the thing it works upon. The land bites deeply into the deep self of the people who live upon it."

Jack D. Rittenhouse is one of the most knowledgeable bookmen in New Mexico. He has been journalist, teacher, editor, book publisher, book printer, winner of close to 50 awards for editorial planning and design, and author of numerous books, including the essential *The Santa Fe Trail: A Historical Bibliography*. Since his retirement as Business Manager and Western Editor of the University of New Mexico Press, Jack and his wife Charlotte have operated an antiquarian book service in Albuquerque.

 22

BOOKSELLING IN TERRITORIAL SANTA FE

Nancy D. May

THE establishment of public schools and the spread of literacy, the arrival of the railroad and the consequent growth of a population that had the extra money to buy books and the leisure time to read them, were late developments in New Mexico. Thus, until the latter part of the nineteenth century, the elements necessary to support the book trade were absent from the region.

Of course there were books in New Mexico before the coming of the railroad in 1879. The Franciscan missionaries and the colonial governors often had small libraries for their personal use brought with them from Spain or Mexico. However, the governors were generally too involved in the problems of maintaining a garrison and protecting the settlements from hostile Indians to promote public education. Nor did the Church, before the efforts of Bishop Lamy, demonstrate any special interest in encouraging literacy. Still, reading was considered the concern of the Church. On at least two occasions that concern prompted the forwarding to Santa Fe of prohibitions against the reading or owning of particular books.

In 1778 an order arrived to burn publicly all copies of a work entitled *Año de 2044*. Governor Chacón, in 1804, was commanded to collect and send to Chihuahua any copies of *Borarquia, o Victima de la Inquisición* and Rousseau's *Social Contract*. Ironically, there was only a small percentage of the population able to read the forbidden works. The majority could neither read nor write and that condition persisted long after New Mexico had become a United States territory. As late as 1890, according to the census, 60% of the area's 160,000 residents were illiterate. But by that time the situation was beginning to improve.

Eleven years earlier the railroad had crossed Raton Pass, and with it had come a wave of settlers whose backgrounds were formed in the public education systems of the States. Among them were Walter V. Hayt, a native New Yorker, and his wife Alice. They settled in Santa Fe and sometime in late 1879 Hayt and a man named Joy opened a store on San Francisco Street. There must have been books among their stock because the following year, on the census, Hayt gave his occupation as "bookseller."

The partnership with Joy was short-lived. By Christmas of 1881 only Hayt's name appeared on the advertisement of "holiday goods" in the *New Mexican*. The goods listed included toys, smoking sets, bronzes, velvet frames, children's books and that interesting innovation of the Victorian publishers—"gift books." By the following spring, Hayt was offering sheet music and drafting and art supplies. In the 1882 *Legislative Blue-Book* he announced that he carried "the most complete stereoscopic views of New Mexico published." While his stock must have included many items of a more practical sort (we know, for example, that he had for sale the *General Laws of New Mexico* at $5.50 a copy), Hayt's advertising clearly reflects a growing market for luxury items and the materials for leisure activities, not the least of which were books.

Although Walter Hayt was the first merchant in Santa Fe, and in the entire territory, to claim the title of bookseller, by the early 1880s other Santa Fe businessmen had begun to answer the demand for books. Mr. E. Andrews —dentist, assayer and jewelry manufacturer— ran a notice in the classified column of the *New Mexican* advising the public that he carried Wilson's revised *History of Santa Fe*. At about the same time H. B. Cartwright advertised himself as the sole agent for *Mill's Handbook of Mining Laws and Guide to New Mexico*.

For several months in 1882 the *New Mexican* promoted the sale of its own production, *The*

Authentic Life of Billy The Kid by Pat Garrett. The newspaper also gave extensive publicity to the first *Legislative Blue-Book*, compiled by W. G. Ritch, Secretary of the Territory. But undoubtedly the most ambitious response to the increasing interest in and need for books, especially within the Spanish-speaking community, came from Felipe B. Delgado.

Delgado operated a general mercantile store on the Plaza from at least 1873 through 1908, the period covered by two of the surviving records of his establishment. In January of 1883 he purchased his first supply of books from a representative of W. A. Rippath, a German publisher. It was a large order consisting of several copies each of fourteen devotional titles in Spanish. There is no further record of books purchased until 1886 when he wrote to Thomas Kelly, location unspecified, in response to a circular offering prayer books at thirteen copies to the dozen with a trade discount of 60%. Two years elapsed before Delgado ordered again. Then, in December of 1888, he wrote the first letter of a twenty year association with Benziger Brothers, a well-established publishing house. At that time there were apparently few, if any, American publishers of Spanish language religious materials. But Benziger was able to supply Delgado with titles directly from Europe. They quickly became his major supplier and remained so through 1908.

26

During the twenty-five years that he stocked books, Delgado ordered over one hundred titles and several of those did come from other publishers. One particularly popular work was *The Ollendorf Method,* a Spanish language English grammar, which he ordered from Appleton in New York. He also corresponded with B. Herder of St. Louis on a few occasions when he needed copies of Mantilla's *Libro de Lectura No. 1,* an elementary Spanish reader. Felipe Delgado never claimed to be a bookseller in the sense that Walter Hayt seems to have understood that occupation. Yet as a general merchandiser meeting the changing needs of his customers he was probably more typical than Hayt, something of a specialist, of the book retailers of the late territorial period.

While the history of books in New Mexico reaches as far back as the sixteenth century *entradas* of the Spanish, the retail handling of books did not become a viable commercial enterprise until after the railroad arrived. After 1879 not only were freight charges lower but also an influx of American settlers, raised in the tradition of public education, created a wider market for books. The Spanish-speaking community was beginning to recognize the need to learn English. The combination of these factors and many others resulted in a very gradual increase in literacy throughout the territory and a more pro-

NEW MEXICO'S EARLIEST KNOWN
BOOK CIRCULAR

In 1883 LeBaron Bradford Prince (1840-1922) wrote *Historical Sketches of New Mexico* and issued this advertising circular. Apparently he financed its publication, with the printing done by Ramsey, Millett & Hudson, at Kansas City, and with publication through Leggat Brothers, New York City. The book was successful enough to go into a second edition in its first year.

Apparently Prince handled much of the distribution of his book within the state, corresponding with bookshops in the larger towns.

L. B. Prince came to New Mexico in 1878 after being appointed chief justice of the territorial supreme court in that year by President Rutherford B. Hayes. He helped revive the Historical Society of New Mexico in 1881 and was its president in 1883. President Benjamin Harrison appointed him governor of New Mexico Territory in 1889.

Prince had at least five other later published works: *The Stone Lions of Cochiti*, a pamphlet (Santa Fe, 1903); *New Mexico's Struggle for Statehood* (Cedar Rapids, 1910); *Spanish Mission Churches of New Mexico* (Cedar Rapids, 1910); *The Student's History of New Mexico* (Denver, 1913); and a revised edition of the latter, *A Concise History of New Mexico* (Cedar Rapids, 1914).

J. D. R.

History of New Mexico.

The long-felt want of some book giving an account of the romantic and interesting events in the history of New Mexico, is at last met by the publication of

"Historical Sketches of New Mexico,"

FROM THE EARLIEST RECORDS TO THE AMERICAN OCCUPATION,

—— B Y ——

L. BRADFORD PRINCE,

President of the Historical Society of New Mexico, late Chief Justice, etc.

The following table of contents will show the scope of the work:

TABLE OF CONTENTS.

THIS VOLUME CONTAINS 328 PAGES, WITH AN APPENDIX.

Price, Bound in Cloth, $2.00.

☞ SENT POST PAID BY MAIL, WITHOUT EXTRA CHARGE.

REGULAR DISCOUNT TO THE TRADE.

Apply to

LEGGAT BROTHERS, Publishers, Chambers Street, **New York**,

Or **L. B. PRINCE**, Santa Fe, **New Mexico.**

[See Notices of the Press on other side]

29

nounced increase in small communities like Santa Fe where the new settlers were concentrated. Thus the 1880s saw the beginnings of the book trade in New Mexico as merchants responded to the increased demand for books to inform or simply to entertain.

———————

Nancy May was working in an Albuquerque bookstore and completing a Master's in English Literature at the University of New Mexico when she became interested in early bookselling in the Southwest. This original contribution on the subject is the result of many hours of research through territorial records and publications of the time.

30

THE TWO MOST ENDURING BOOK SHOPS IN NEW MEXICO

Justine Thomas & Claire Morrill with Genevieve Janssen

THE OLDEST bookstore in New Mexico that is still vitally involved in serving a segment of New Mexico's population is Villagrá Book Shop of Santa Fe. It was started by Roberta Robey in the early 1920s in a corner of another shop that was located on the east side of the Plaza, next to the present-day Packard's Indian Trading Company. It was Roberta Robey's good friend, the poet Alice Corbin Henderson, who suggested the name "Villagrá Book Shop" as a tribute to Gaspar Pérez de Villagrá, poet and historian who traveled with Don Juan de Oñate. Villagrá wrote the first history of New Mexico in 1610, published as *Historia de la Nueva México* in Alcalé de Henares, Spain.

The book shop remained at its Plaza location until 1928, when it moved to the Sena building. This beautiful old building, surrounding a large central courtyard, was built in 1831 as the home of Major José D. Sena. It had been purchased from the Sena family by Amalia White and her sister Elizabeth, who engaged William

Penlow Henderson to remodel it. Thus, in 1927, a second story was added on the north and east sides and a portal added to what became the "business front" facing Palace Avenue. The White sisters were dedicated bibliophiles, owners of the famous Howell-Lincoln book collection, which was ultimately willed to the School of American Research, along with the Sena building. In 1980 the School of American Research sold the building to a private enterprise.

During the 1930s Spud Johnson and Robert Hunt were the managers of the Villagrá Book Shop. The shop was already a landmark for literary New Mexico. Noted national authors such as Mary Austin, Willa Cather, Robert Frost, Carl Sandburg, Oliver LaFarge, Paul Horgan, Frieda Lawrence and Mable Luhan, to name but a few, visited and shopped in the cosy bookstore with its fireplace and its famous and all-too-comfortable chair, which is now in the home of Carla Thomas, daughter of Justine Thomas. Every afternoon at four, La Fonda hotel sent over a tray of martinis, and whoever was in the store at that time joined with such as Upton Sinclair or Thornton Wilder for a late afternoon drink. In 1936 the book shop published *From The Royal City* by Paul Horgan (printed by the Rydal Press).

In the mid-1940s Dorothy Greenwood purchased the shop and it began to look more like a book shop. Nancy Lane bought the shop in 1956 and added even more bookshelves in the one cramped room. Villagrá changed owners again in 1966 when Roslyn Eisenberg and Justine Thomas acquired it from Nancy Lane. The famous chair was finally removed, and the fireplace was forever cooled, in an effort to use every available spot to put in more books. Justine continued the tradition of "bookseller turned author" when Sunstone Press published her *Santa Fe, The City Different.* The current owner, Nancy Applegate, is under contract to write her first book, with Santa Fe again the major subject.

Nancy Applegate purchased the store in January 1978. Her father, George Applegate, worked with her until his death in November 1980. Though the shop moved in the spring of 1981, it is not far from its old location—just fifty-one steps up the portal at the east end of the Sena building. Here in expanded quarters, under the original *vigas,* Villagrá Book Shop continues to dispense books and hospitality as it has done through the years.

It was in 1947 that Genevieve Janssen and Claire Morrill came clattering over the mountain passes from Raton to set up a book shop in Taos. It was quite a switch for both of them. Claire had been managing editor of a daily newspaper in the industrial-chemical center of Midland, Michigan, and Genevieve had been a psychiatric social worker. After seventeen years on the newspaper job, Claire began to wish for a more serene life, closer to the belles-lettres and aesthetic. Genevieve had been delighted with her profession, which brought her to the graduate school of the University of Oklahoma, teaching psychiatric case work.

At the end of World War II they planned to take a year off together to see some country outside the United States. But the world was still war-oriented; you could not move around in Europe and Asia unless you were on business or were willing to be led around by the hearty hand of a tour director. Too frustrated by all this, they looked around for new pastures, Claire for a permanent thing, Genevieve for at least a brief fling.

How about a book shop in some place with verve and color? Fine, but what place? About this time they began to hear about Taos, from faculty friends and a spread in *Holiday Magazine*. If it was half as good as it sounded, Taos was the place. Claire was sent to scout the area. Taos, she found, was an art center, oriented to aesthetics, and set in one of the world's great beauty spots. But Taos was small and poor. It was, in short, a wonderful place to lose your shirt. But they could not resist it.

 34

They set up the book shop from scratch in an alcove of a curio shop on the Plaza. Three years later they moved it to The Mission Shop on Kit Carson Street, following the death of Ralph Meyers, who for thirty years had operated it as a distinguished Indian trading post. It was a magnificent 150 year old adobe building, with its thick walls hung with old Indian cradleboards, old wooden saddles and Indian beaded artifacts. Books settled comfortably into this setting, since they specialized in New Mexicana, whether new, scarce or rare. To this were added general books: color plate volumes in fields allied with the arts; contemporary fiction and non-fiction; children's books and carefully chosen paperbacks. The Taos Book Shop continued to strengthen its interest in serving the wants and needs of individual customers. As a result it got book requests from all parts of the United States, searched for out-of-print Southwestern Americana, and had a mailing list carefully kept pared to 2,000 names. It got a strong response to occasional brief out-of-print book catalogs and its annual pre-Christmas publication, *The Taos Book Shop News*, which is still highly informal and Taos oriented today.

Then in 1972 they had to move again. This was sad news for them as they felt that the old Mission Shop was the ideal setting for the Taos Book Shop. But it proved to be the best thing that could have happened. They were just plain lucky, because, for the first time in more than thirty years, the beautiful old building that had housed the Blue Door Gallery became available. It was located only a few doors away and had three times the space they had previously, plus a charming patio, three fireplaces and a marvelous view of Taos Mountain. It was really perfect.

With the move they decided it was time to sell books and only books. For twenty-two years they had enjoyed selling fine Indian jewelry, vegetable dye rugs, kachinas and many unusual Indian artifacts. It was difficult to give up their buying trips to the Navajo, Hopi and Zuni reservations, but their first and lasting interest was in selling books.

In December 1973 the University of New Mexico Press published Claire's beautiful book, *A Taos Mosaic*, with many photographs by Laura Gilpin. The autographing party they had for the book was a great success and in many ways was the highlight of their book shop years.

In January 1975 the Taos Book Shop was sold to Professor and Mrs. Paul Wilson and to Professors Walter and Sally Sedelow, faculty members of Kansas University. Since that time there have been further changes in ownership, but the Taos Book Shop still carries on most of the traditions that were started back in 1947. The shop has been an important cultural insti-

36

tution in Taos for many years. They didn't lose their shirts—instead they had a wonderful life in the Taos Book Shop and most of their customers became their friends.

Justine Thomas now lives a busy life of retirement in Santa Fe, where for many years she was the dean of booksellers. She has written many articles and a long-favorite book that describes her beloved Santa Fe. Roslyn Eisenberg continues to teach at the New Mexico School for the Deaf in Santa Fe.

Claire Morrill's death in June of 1980 came two months before her 82nd birthday. Her lifelong friend and partner, Genevieve Janssen, now lives in Ranchos de Taos. The story here related about the Taos Book Shop was taken from an article written by Claire for *Book Talk* in July 1972.

These four beautiful women gave succor to fledgling authors for many years when they dominated the bookselling scene in New Mexico. Their stores were truly literary havens for the accomplished author or the penny-poor book buyer. They remain our models as totally involved booksellers.

BOOKS WERE SCARCE IN COLONIAL
NEW MEXICO

Marc Simmons

IN 1917 A New Mexican sheepherder wandered into a cave in the Ladron Mountains west
of Socorro and made a rare discovery. On the
floor of the cave, he found an ancient Spanish
trunk, built of wood and covered with rawhide.
Inside was a collection of six books, all printed
before 1600. The volumes included two Bibles.
One was in Greek, dated 1596, and another in
Hebrew, 1584. Then there was a book of medi-
eval sermons and also a book of verse, containing a poem on the silkworm and another poem
on the game of chess. Also among the printed
treasures was a Spanish edition (1548) of the Roman author Petrarch's *Triunfos*.

The fact that all the books had been published in the 1500s suggests that they were probably brought to New Mexico with Juan de
Oñate's great colonizing expedition of 1598. On
the blank leaf of one of the volumes a padre had
written in ink his name and the date: Fray Diego
Jiménez, 1679. This tells us that the books were
left in the cave sometime after that.

[38]

Quite probably the trunk and its contents were stolen from some mission library during the Pueblo Indian revolt of 1680. The Apaches joined with the Pueblos in the uprising and since the Ladron Mountains was one of their favorite haunts, we can guess it was they who hauled the trunk there and left it in the cave. There must have been other booty that the Apaches carried away, but the books were abandoned because they couldn't think of any way to use them.

Books of any kind were a rarity on New Mexico's Spanish colonial frontier. The few volumes that did manage to travel up the Camino Real from Mexico City, Zacatecas, Durango and Chihuahua had a rough time of it. Weather, insects, Indian raids and simple human neglect took their toll. Scarcely any of those original books survive today. Even those found in that cave in 1917 have since mysteriously disappeared. The trunk that protected them for several centuries was sold to a collector in Chicago.

The missionaries and the royal governors were about the only ones who could boast of any kind of library. The padres usually kept a variety of religious books on hand to aid them in teaching the Indians. We do know that at the mission of Santo Domingo Pueblo just north of Albuquerque, the priests there had a collection of more than 250 volumes in 1776. Besides devotional works, there were Spanish histories, grammars, dictionaries and Latin classics.

New Mexico's great soldier and governor, Don Diego de Vargas, brought several cases of books with him from El Paso when he marched up the Rio Grande in 1693 to resettle the province after the Pueblo revolt. Upon his death in 1704 during an Indian campaign, Vargas willed his valuable collection of books to his children.

Another Spanish governor who owned a library was Bernardo López de Mendizabal. His wife, Doña Teresa, who came from Mexico City, was bored with life in provincial Santa Fe, so she spent much of her time reading. One of her favorite works was a romantic novel, *Orlando Furioso,* written in Italian. It was a perfectly harmless book, of course. But gossips and busybodies in Santa Fe whispered that the novel, since it was in a foreign language, must be full of heresies against the Church. They denounced poor Doña Teresa before agents of the Inquisition. As a result of these trumped-up charges, the governor's wife was arrested, sent in chains to Mexico City, and tossed into the dungeons of the Inquisition. It was several years before she could prove her innocence and gain her freedom.

A few private individuals in New Mexico did on occasion own a handful of books. One was a colonist named Juan del Caso Barona who came with Oñate in 1598. His occupation was listed as that of barber and surgeon. Records show that he had "five medical books by recognized authorities." His small collection may well represent the first medical library in any part of the present United States.

Most citizens, it would seem, stayed away from books. Part of the answer was that they simply couldn't read. But for those who could, fear of the Inquisition discouraged book buying. The fate of the hapless Doña Teresa offered a stern warning.

I have seen Spanish documents, still preserved in the Santa Fe archives, ordering the governor to confiscate all books which contain heresies or revolutionary ideas. Among them is a decree from the King, dated 1803. It refers to the depraved writings of the French author Rousseau. His books, the decree says, contain liberty slogans and advocate independence, and they are designed "to destroy the Spanish throne and altar." The governor is instructed to seize any of Rousseau's works he can find and send them to Chihuahua under lock and key, so that nobody will be able to read them on the road going south.

Another book received even harsher treatment. It was a volume published in London under the title *The Year 2044*. That sounds like an early-day work of science fiction. Whatever its contents, the King decided it was dangerous. He sent a letter to the governor in Santa Fe advising him to seize and burn any copies that might have slipped into the New Mexican settlements. But I'm sure he needn't have bothered. There is no evidence whatever that even a single copy of *The Year 2044* ever got anywhere near the Rio Grande Valley.

Marc Simmons is probably the only professional farrier in the Southwest with a Ph.D. in history. He has written many books of vital interest to the Southwesterner, and the continual flow from his pen appears in newspapers, magazines and journals so frequently that we are inclined to believe that there must be more than one scholar behind all this work. He now lives in Cerrillos in an adobe house he built himself.

FRONTIER BOOK AND STATIONERY
SALESMAN

Paul J. Wielandy

AT THE AGE of 19 I began my career as a traveling salesman for Shorb & Boland of St. Louis, then the largest book and stationery jobbing house west of the Mississippi River. I was assigned the territory west of the Rockies, including the Territory of New Mexico. On January 13, 1883, I started on my maiden trip calling on Otero, Sellar & Co., who were doing construction work for the Santa Fe Railroad, which was blazing its way through New Mexico. The trip was made by sled in below zero weather, with my five sample trunks in the wagon bed, to see A. M. Blackwell, purchasing agent of the construction company. I succeeded in selling him a huge order.

About once a year I would go to Española, via the Chile Line, and from Española take the stage to Santa Fe. The Chile Line was a little 90 mile branch which ran a tri-weekly mixed passenger and freight train from Antonito, Colorado, to Española, New Mexico, the terminus. Bond Brothers store was the only one in the

little town (of Española) and they carried everything, as the saying goes, from a needle to a
windmill. There were no hotels in Española,
but comfortable accommodations were to be had
at the home of Mrs. Burns, the wife of the section foreman. Two whiskey drummers, Sam
Cohen of Frisco and Henry Essinger of St. Joe,
were along with me on this trip. The next morning when we awakened the country was covered with a two foot blanket of snow, and as it
was impossible for the stage to cross the Pass to
Santa Fe, we were in for an enforced rest.

One evening, while snowbound, George
Bond asked me to go a few rounds with Pistol
Johnny, the stage driver. At that time I was pret-
ty handy with my dukes and always carried a
set of boxing gloves in my sample trunks. When
we stepped into the improvised ring, it didn't
take me long to get Pistol Johnny's measure. I
played around a little while but, when I got the
old zinger on him, he went down like the old
oaken bucket. It was no credit to kayo Pistol
Johnny, as he was at least 20 years my senior,
but if he could have had his way that night the
doctors would have had a job digging for lead
pellets in my carcass. Pistol Johnny, whose right
name was John W. Fewel, and I became lasting
friends.

Raton, New Mexico, was a trading point for
cattlemen before the Santa Fe Railroad tapped

44

it and this is where Fred Harvey established the first of his chain of railroad eating houses in New Mexico and Arizona. My principal customer in Raton was a St. Louis boy named Joe Schroeter, who was the owner of a drug and stationery store. On one of my spring trips from Raton to Springer, I met Bob Ingersoll who was bound for Senator Elkins' ranch near Springer. About four months later, while booking an order in Kremis' Drug Store at Springer, Col., Ingersoll came in to make a little purchase and seemed delighted to see me. When he learned that I was selling books and stationery he asked Mr. Kremis if he could have a conference with me. He wanted me to fit him out with about $500. worth of books for a library which he wanted to give to the Senator and left the selection to me. The order was shipped through Mr. Kremis and the Colonel wrote me an appreciative letter.

Forty miles south of Springer is Wagon Mound, another cattle and sheep trading point. John Justus Schmidt, one of the grandest merchants in the Territory, was proprietor of the only general store in this peaceful little cattle and sheep town. In 1892 on one of my trips, I learned about a week before I arrived that Mr. Schmidt had been assassinated by José Gallegos, whom he had befriended. The brutal murder was on account of some trouble over a herd of sheep.

45

About 30 miles north of Las Vegas is Mora. Bob Schulteis, an old pal representing a St. Louis saddlery house, traveled in the same territory I covered and we doubled up to save expenses on this trip. A merchant from Taos whom Bob had never met was in the market for a bill of goods and he had written Bob to meet him at Mora during court session. Tom Walton, proprietor of the Walton Palacio and a gambling house, was an all around good hombre. He told us he had only one 3-bed room left and asked us to share the room with someone who might arrive. About 10 p.m. a nice looking chap was assigned to our room. After exchanging a little pleasantry, we assured him we would get along fine and dandy. The stranger laid his Colt .45 on the table and began to disrobe. Bob and I did the same but we were rehearsing the hot reception "Mr. Badman" would receive if he showed up that night.

Our roommate began to squirm and asked us if we were expecting trouble. We told him not exactly trouble, but there was a bad egg in town and if he learned we were in this hotel our goose was cooked. It wasn't long until our roommate grabbed his six-shooter and pulled stakes. Bob and I went to bed. The next morning Tom Walton spied us at the breakfast table and asked us what in the world we had done to old Juan Santistevan, the big merchant from Taos? When Bob heard the name, he really was fit to be tied as Juan Santistevan was the man whom Bob expected to meet at Mora.

Forty miles west of Watrous is the old Spanish town of Las Vegas. The town was divided by the Gallinas River. It is here where Jacob Gross, the office man, Harry Kelly, and A. M. Blackwell, the purchasing agent for Otero, Sellar & Co., took over the merchandise stock of the company when they completed their construction contract with the Santa Fe. Gross, Blackwell & Co. became the biggest jobbers of merchandise and the largest handlers of wool in the territory. Browne, Manzaneres & Co. were also a big concern and competition between the two firms was always most pleasant.

In the old town of Las Vegas adjoining the Plaza Hotel, Charles Ilfeld & Co. was located. They dealt principally in dry goods and notions. In 1885 I stopped at the Plaza Hotel to display my holiday line of samples. One morning as I came to breakfast the clerk said, "Paul, walk up a block and you'll behold a sight!" On the limb of a big cottonwood dangled the bodies of three tough looking hombres—horse thieves hung by the vigilante committee. One of the show places of Las Vegas was the grand Montezuma Hotel, built by the Santa Fe. I was fortunate upon one occasion to be one of the dinner guests there of Miguel Otero's father. Las Vegas had a daily newspaper which became

47

quite famous on account of its witty and live wire editor, Russ Kistler.

Santa Fe was my favorite town when I was a young traveling salesman in the '80s. I would plan to spend Sunday there so I could enjoy a rest at the Palace Hotel, which served meals unexcelled by any hotel west of St. Louis. Many times I have enjoyed the concerts furnished by the band from Fort Marcy in the historical Plaza.

In Albuquerque, the Santa Fe railroad station was located about a mile east of the original town. The hotels, restaurants, gambling houses and stores were centered in close proximity to the railway station, and business in the old town was on the decline. About the only thing left in the way of business in old Albuquerque was Huning's big general merchandise store, which could be reached by a little dinky street car line pulled over narrow gauge tracks by a burro.

I would stop at Belen twice a year where John Becker, a big merchant, was located. The town was about a mile west of the railway station, and a brother of John Becker was the station agent and owner of a little adobe building in which a traveler could get sleeping accommodations. Socorro, a lively silver mining camp about 60 miles south of Belen, had just heard that the Apaches had swooped down on a caravan of freighters headed for the mining camps of Magdalena and Kelly, 20-some miles west, and had killed three drivers and badly wounded another. They were organizing a posse of business men to run them down and, as I wouldn't be able to do any business until their return, I was induced to join them. Believe you me, when we got back to Socorro without success, we were the most fatigued, down-and-out, hungry-looking specimens you ever saw; but after a good night's rest I was ready to book orders.

Lake Valley was a town of less than 100 people, but it was a big trading post for ranchmen and miners and the terminus of a little branch road on the Santa Fe. While I was booking an order at the big store in Lake Valley, Jim Cox, the livery man, dropped in and inquired what time I would be ready to leave the next morning for Kingston. But, Mr. Keller, my customer, told me I would be taking an awful chance because of the Apaches and that everyone was hugging close to their homes. This knocked out my idea of going to Kingston, so I took the train for Rincon, a junction of the Santa Fe, where passengers had to change going to and from El Paso, Deming and Silver City.

On my first trip to Deming in 1883, the pioneers were building the town and it was called a town of tents—the outskirts being covered with acres of army tents to accommodate U.S.

49

government troops in command of General Crook. They had been stationed there to put an end to the murderous warfare of the Apaches. Deming could boast of only a few substantial adobe buildings among which was a large general merchandise store, S. Lindauer & Co. The drummer who was lucky to be first on the job after the Mexican traders and smugglers gutted the stores would book real orders.

In the early '80s the price of silver bullion ran from $1.10 to $1.29 per ounce, making silver mining extremely profitable. Silver City began to boom. It was in 1886 that John J. Pershing served as 2nd Lieutenant of the 6th Cavalry in the U.S. Army, stationed at Fort Bayard near Silver City. I met Lt. Pershing upon several occasions in the drug store of Colonel W. C. Porterfield who later commanded the Second Volunteer Regiment of New Mexico during the Spanish War.

I saw Silver City at the height of its boom, when silver bullion reached its peak. Everybody was on his toes piling up money and spending it about as fast as he made it. Price never entered into a sale. No mining camp had the slappity bang of Silver City during the days of the 1880s. It was here that I accidently met Calamity Jane, a familiar character known in every booming camp. She was a battle-axe to be sure, but the old gal was far from being washed up and she was an artist at squeezing cards in a poker game. Poker Alice Tubbs was another picturesque character of the Old West. She carried a pistol, smoked cigars, swore like a trooper and also was an inveterate poker player. One evening she took $6,000. at one night's sitting at Silver City.

In those boom mining camps it was "all day in the day time and no night at all"—there were no locks on doors of stores, saloons and gambling dives. Women of easy virtue, the "gold diggers," would flock to boom camps and cowtowns. Babies and children were not in evidence —there were no schools and but few churches. The law lay in a holster on a man's thigh; and the honored judge was generally the best gunman. Horse thieves and cattle rustlers were considered of the deepest dye. Hemp stretching parties were a common occurrence.

I love that country—New Mexico is close to my heart. I would love to live my life all over again in the Old West where all men are virile and quick on the draw and dearly would I love to shake my old friends by their paw. Yes, I wish I could face about and see my humble footprints in the business sand—out in New Mexico, the most fascinating country in the land.

———

Used by permission of the *New Mexico Magazine*, based on articles appearing in the July and August, 1949 issues.

NEW MEXICO'S FIRST PRINTER,

And Seven Who Followed

Jack D. Rittenhouse

PRINTING brings cohesion to society. The arrival of a printing press changes an outpost into a city. It democratizes learning by making it accessible to all. Each city, each region has dates that mark its birth and progress, and one of the most significant rites of passage is the arrival of the first printing press. From that point onward all is different, in part because the press had arrived.

A first press is followed by others, of course, and most of the newcomers do more or less the same kind of printing: newspapers, pamphlets, and legal or business work. The years pass and then comes a flowering of culture as new craftsmen set up their type cases to experiment with other uses of the printed word. They publish material with a different content; they search for better design, adding beauty to utility; they serve new writers who seek new audiences.

In New Mexico the first printing press arrived in 1834. Within the next hundred years, plus perhaps a decade, seven other unusual printing houses arose in New Mexico and in the lands adjacent. This is a summary of the first and the seven who followed.

THE MARTINEZ PRESS

Padre Antonio José Martínez was the first book publisher in New Mexico. His first book was a little speller entitled *Cuaderno de Ortografía,* printed late in 1834 when the *padre* was forty-one. A printing press had been in New Mexico less than six months, and the story of that equipment is still being verified and corrected. Each succeeding account differs a little from previous versions, as fact replaces hearsay and as verification alters conjecture. At this moment the story stands about as follows:

In 1831 there was apparently no press in New Mexico but New Mexicans knew that they needed one. In that year in Mexico City Antonio Barreiro was appointed *asesor* and was sent north to Santa Fe. The council in Santa Fe that year wrote a proposal to change New Mexico into the State of Hidalgo. Their proposal was unsuccessful, but its text included a comment that "when the revenues of the State will permit, a printing-press and outfit will be purchased."

Four men in Santa Fe played roles in the advent of printing in the state: Barreiro; Ramón Abreu, a man of some wealth and then the pro-

53

vincial secretary; the priest Martínez; and Josiah Gregg, a young American who had arrived in July, 1831, on his first trip west over the Santa Fe Trail. Gregg stayed in New Mexico more than a year on his first visit.

In 1832 Barreiro wrote a description of New Mexico, published that year in Puebla with the title *Ojeada sobre Nuevo Méjico,* in which he mentioned that there was no printing press in the state. Josiah Gregg wrote later in his *Commerce of the Prairies* (1844) that "there never has been a single newspaper or periodical of any kind published in New Mexico except in the year 1834. . ." Barreiro and Gregg thus seem to quiet any claims for other presses, such as one rumored to have been at the colony proposed by John Heath north of El Paso around 1823. Heath may have shipped a press to Mexico to be hauled north, but the colony was not built and no equipment arrived.

Gregg went back to Missouri in the fall of 1833 and eventually became a great trader over the Santa Fe Trail. It is reasonable to assume that he was aware that some people in Santa Fe wanted a press. In a Missouri newspaper, the *Republican,* there was an advertisement that winter, on February 10, 1834, that Samuel Dickinson [*sic*] in Cincinnati had new and used printing presses for sale, so Gregg would have known where to get a press.

We do know how and when a press reached Santa Fe. Historian Max Moorhead, who wrote *New Mexico's Royal Road*, found the facts in a document in the Archivo Histórico de Hacienda (Legajo 176-3) in Mexico City. It contained a freight manifest of the trading partners Joseph Sutton and Josiah Gregg recorded at the port of entry: *Manifiesto de José Sutton y Josiah Gregg, Santa Fe, 29 de Julio de 1834,* listing a printing press and equipment. Moorhead thus wiped out any conjectures that the 1834 press came from Guaymas or Chihuahua. It came over the Santa Fe Trail and reached Santa Fe on July 29, 1834.

The bibliographic historian Henry Raup Wagner and printing historian Douglas McMurtrie believe the press was of the style known as a Ramage press. Gregg described it as a "very small press" that printed a "foolscap sheet." Folded once, a foolscap sheet is roughly the size of what we now call legal size paper. Examination of the sizes of known specimens done on the 1834 press shows that the greatest width of the paper page was 8 1/2 inches and the greatest length was 13 1/2 inches, and this matches Gregg's description.

The Ramage press was a simplified version using the general principles of presses used by Gutenberg and Franklin, and its frame and lever action were similar to those of the Washington handpress. The type page was placed on a slid-

55

ing horizontal flat bed, with the characters facing up. The type was inked and a sheet of paper laid on it, and the bed was then slid under an upper flat surface, the platen. When a lever was pulled, the platen pressed down on the sheet and the type was printed on the paper. The platen was then lifted, the bed pulled out, the sheet removed and the process repeated.

Upon its arrival in Santa Fe, the press became the property of Ramón Abreu, and this is verified by a statement on the earliest known example from this press. A printer was on hand to operate the equipment: Jesús María Baca, from Durango, Mexico. He remained with the press for many years, and what we know of him comes from the obituary that appeared in the Santa Fe *New Mexican* when he died on April 24, 1876.

We do not know how or why Baca came to Santa Fe. He could have been asked to come by Abreu or Barreiro or Martínez; he could have been there already. Perhaps Gregg had notified Abreu that he was bringing a press, allowing Abreu to summon a pressman. Martínez had spent some time in Durango and may have met Baca, but when Martínez left Durango in 1823 there were no printers in Durango, nor did Martínez return there at any time in the early 1830s. Historian Lansing Bloom believed that Barreiro summoned Baca, but Barreiro may have been acting for Abreu in the matter.

 56

The press was put to immediate use upon its arrival. Under a Mexican law of October 14, 1828, on freedom of the press, Abreu went through the required steps to open a printing operation. An *aviso* or notice of intent to operate a printing establishment was printed and posted. Next a panel of jurymen, or *jurado de la imprenta*, was drawn up, consisting of fifty men who could read and write and who owned at least 4,000 pesos or who had an annual income of 400 pesos from some legitimate profession or trade. A list of these was printed on August 14, 1834, and copies of this *Lista de Ciudadanos* remain as the first known examples of the first known printing in New Mexico. The jury would sit on any case involving the printer.

After these required preliminaries, printing began in earnest. The first work published appears to have been a periodical or sort of campaign newspaper, *El Crepúsculo de la Libertad* (The Dawn of Liberty), printed at Santa Fe sometime between late August and early October, 1834. The historical accounts that mention a number specify a series of four issues. It was published to aid the political campaign of Antonio Barreiro who sought and won election to the Mexican Congress.

No copy of this periodical has been found, not even a fragment or facsimile or reproduction, so we know nothing of its design or content except that it probably was a single sheet of foolscap paper folded to make four pages, approximately equal to modern legal size. Josiah Gregg, who probably saw a copy, said that it was "issued for about a month, to the tune of fifty subscribers." According to the minutes of the *ayuntamiento* at Santa Fe, Barreiro filed a set of all issues with that council on October 8, 1834. In a letter to the council on January 17, 1835, Ramón Abreu asked that the body "exhibit in its session hall a file of the periodical *Crepúsculo de la Libertad*..." Another letter sent soon afterward from Santa Fe to Mexico City mentioned that the writer was enclosing a set of all issues.

Before the end of 1834 Padre Martínez had a small spelling book done on the equipment, although Martínez did not personally own the press or do the presswork. This *Cuaderno de Ortografía* is generally credited as being the first book printed in New Mexico. It was a pocket-size pamphlet. In 1929 Douglas McMurtrie did a facsimile of it for the John Calhoun Club in Chicago. Copies of this keepsake turn up occasionally, consisting of two small booklets in a slipcase with the label *First Printing in New Mexico*.

In 1835 Padre Martínez secured full use of the press and took it up to Taos. The printer José María Baca went with him. From that time on the press became known as the Martínez press, although it may have belonged to the Abreu family. Padre Martínez had the required *aviso* published in Taos, along with the list of jurymen. A copy of that *aviso* survives. Perhaps because the press had been known as the one on which Barreiro's *El Crepúsculo* was printed in Santa Fe, the legend grew that Martínez printed the same newspaper in Taos. There are only two bits of evidence supporting this, both doubtful. The obituary of Baca, on his death in 1876, mentioned that he had helped Martínez print *El Crepúsculo* in Taos. Hasty newspaper obituaries are not always accepted fully by competent historians, but this shaky bit of evidence seems to have started a succession of historians' comments on the Taos newspaper, each citing his or her predecessor but with no other proof of any kind. These included H. H. Bancroft, L. Bradford Prince, Benjamin Read, R. E. Twitchell, James Coan, Lansing Bloom and Blanche Grant. In Read's case, a newspaper account in 1916 said he had seen a copy of the Taos newspaper but none was found among his papers. A newspaper was started in Taos in 1917 and was named *Taos Valley News and El Crepúsculo*. The first newspaper in Taos was the *Taos Valley Mirror*, started in 1878. But until a copy of the earlier paper is actually found, or other firm evidence appears, and we hope it does, it must be assumed that the paper was printed only in Santa Fe.

59

This is not to discredit Padre Martínez, who alone in New Mexico in 1834 grasped the educational possibilities of the printing press. He wrote and published a series of small books on spelling, arithmetic, rhetoric, and religious matters, as well as a series of broadsides, folders, and leaflets presenting his position on issues of the day. The press was sent back to Santa Fe at various times in the following years, for other printing. The largest and most valuable item was the *Kearny Code,* printed soon after the arrival of American troops at Santa Fe in 1846.

Padre Martínez died in 1867. Some few years before he had turned the printing equipment over to another. At present the most active researcher into the full history of the Martínez press is Pamela Smith, head of the Palace Press at the Museum of New Mexico in Santa Fe.

LAGUNA MISSION PRESS

One of the next unusual printing establishments in New Mexico was operated between 1877 and 1889 by a Presbyterian missionary at Laguna Pueblo, where the Rev. John Menaul had his Laguna Mission Press. Information on this press is scarce, fragmentary, and sometimes contradictory, because some writers confuse John Menaul with his brother James, also a Presbyterian missionary who was sent to the Navajos in 1870.

In 1876 the Rev. John Menaul was sent to Laguna Pueblo to revive a mission school that had become inactive. He learned the Queres (Keres) language of the pueblo and soon acquired a Washington-style handpress and type. Apparently Menaul did the typesetting and presswork himself. Later he acquired a better job press.

The most interesting and most valuable item from the Laguna Mission Press was its "edition" of a McGuffey's Reader. To make the book useful in his Laguna classes, Menaul translated high points of many lessons into the Laguna tongue, set the type, and printed interleaves for the books. He had acquired several copies of McGuffey's *New First Eclectic Reader* and took them to a bookbinder in Albuquerque, so the interleaves could be bound in. Only three copies are known, one being an imperfect copy at the Southwest Museum in Los Angeles and another in the library of the Museum of the American Indian in New York City. In 1976 I acquired the only known set of proofsheets of these interleaves, and they are now in the Special Collections at the University of New Mexico library.

William G. Ritch wrote in 1882 that Menaul had also started a weekly Spanish newspaper, *La Solona* [*sic*], at Laguna in 1878. Not a single copy survives to confirm this. Menaul also translated some religious lessons and printed them for classroom use. He also printed reports for his Presbyterian superiors back east, describing the needs and accomplishments of his Laguna mission.

When L. Bradford Prince wrote his *Concise History of New Mexico* in 1914 he mentioned the Laguna Mission Press and even at that date described the Menaul pamphlets as "very rare." Rare-book libraries such as the Huntington, the Newberry, University of New Mexico and the Museum of New Mexico each hold a few examples, as does this writer.

It appears that the printing equipment was moved to Albuquerque around 1889, and Rev. Menaul used it there to print religious tracts in Spanish. But his Laguna work was some of the first Indian language printing done on the spot at any pueblo in New Mexico.

THE BANDAR LOG PRESS

One of the terms hardest to define in the world of books is the phrase "private press." There is fairly wide agreement on the part of the definition that says that a private press reflects the selection, taste and effort of one person or a small group of persons who place great emphasis on the design and appearance of the book. Before 1900 all printing in the Southwest was purely utilitarian, with the mechanical work done in a craftsmanlike style but with a taste that was pure, plain vanilla. The first private press in the Southwest, in a design sense, was the Bandar Log Press that existed in Phoenix from 1902 to 1904.

Frank Holme was born in West Virginia in 1868 and became an artist. At the age of seventeen he was working as a newspaper illustrator in the days when many news stories carried sketches instead of photographs. His drawings of the Johnstown Flood disaster brought him fame and an offer of a job on a Chicago newspaper. There, as a hobby, he acquired printing equipment and began his Bandar Log Press in Chicago in 1895, naming the press for the monkey people in Kipling's *The Jungle Book,* whose attention switched constantly from one new interest to another. He worked prodigiously, attracted friends easily, improved his art skills, and in 1901 found himself worn out and seriously ill with tuberculosis. He went to North Carolina for a year and did one or two books on his private press before his physician ordered him to Arizona in 1902.

Holme was without capital or income. A friend "incorporated" the Bandar Log Press by organizing a hundred "stockholders" who took shares at twenty-five dollars each. Holme offered to repay them with dividends in the form of handprinted books.

These books, of which six or seven known

63

titles were printed in Phoenix in editions ranging from 174 to 674 copies, were truly handcrafted. Holme hand set the type, drew the illustrations and carved them on woodblocks, and did the presswork on a Washington-style handpress.

Of the books he did in Phoenix, the most famous is his *Poker Rubaiyat*, embellished with multicolor illustrations that required a total of a hundred and six hand-cut blocks. Its cover measures about eight by ten inches, and some illustrations are in as many as nine colors. Another outstanding work is *Her Navajo Lover*, done in 1903 as the last book printed by Frank Holme and the first book written by Will Robinson, who later wrote *Under Turquoise Skies*.

At Phoenix, Holme's press was at the Schrogl Ranch, on what is now the Black Canyon highway about three and a half miles from the center of Phoenix. At the ranch were several tents housing invalids. The printing equipment was in a converted chicken coop.

Although there are many stories about invalids who came west and lived to an old age, such was not the lot of Frank Holme. He died in Denver in 1904 at the age of thirty-six. His greatest fan was Edwin Hill, who organized a correspondence group of Frank Holme enthusiasts to swap recollections through an occasional bulletin until Hill died in 1949. The Hill collection of Holme material is now at the Henry

E. Huntington Library. The University of Arizona Library has a full set of Holme's books, but they are so scarce that few other Southwestern libraries hold any copies.

THE FIRST COWBOY SONG BOOK

America's first book of cowboy songs was printed in a small weekly newspaper shop in Estancia, New Mexico, in 1908. It was N. Howard Thorp's *Songs of the Cowboys*.

Nathan Howard Thorp, usually known as Jack Thorp, was born in the east and came west as a youth. When he was twenty-two he began to jot down the words of songs he heard on the cattle ranges, and later he tried his own hand at writing songs. Many of the tunes were based on the music of popular ballads or old revival hymns.

In 1903 Jack married Annette Hesch and settled on her father's sheep ranch at Palma, east of Albuquerque along what later became U. S. Route 66 and not far from present Estancia. Estancia was a bustling town in those ranch and homestead days. Its first newspaper was *Las Nuevas de la Estancia,* started in 1904 and bought out by P. A. Speckman in 1907, when it was renamed the weekly *Estancia News.* By 1909 the town had four newspapers and was at its crest; by late 1912 the village was back to only one paper, the *News.*

In 1908 Thorp decided to put the songs into

a book. He rode into Estancia and "made a dicker" with the *Estancia News* to print two thousand copies, paying six cents a copy or $120 for the entire edition. The fifty-page, saddle-stitched pamphlet had a red paper cover with the words *Songs of the Cowboy* / N. Howard Thorp / News Print Shop / Estancia, New Mexico. To embellish the cover, the printer used one of those stock cuts showing the silhouette of a steer, about an inch wide and used by early newspapers when printing cattle brand notices, except that this one had no brand scratched into the metal. The book contained twenty-three songs, with no music, including five songs written by Thorp. His own most famous song was "Little Joe, the Wrangler."

Thorp ran an advertisement in some Kansas newspapers offering the book for fifty cents and eventually sold the entire edition. By 1940, when he described the incident in an article in the August *Atlantic Monthly*, copies were selling in the rare book market for $25. By 1966 the going price was up to $100. By 1975 the price was $1,000; it was $1,350 in 1980.

In 1910 the noted folklorist John A. Lomax published his first book, *Cowboy Songs and Other Frontier Ballads*, through Sturgis and Walton in New York City. Lomax grew in stature as the premier collector of rangeland folksongs, but Jack Thorp was always recognized as the first.

 66

In 1921 Houghton Mifflin Company issued an enlarged edition of *Songs of the Cowboys,* bound in half cloth and paper over boards, with an introduction by Alice Corbin Henderson. In 1926 Thorp issued his privately printed *Tales of the Chuck Wagon* done at Santa Fe. In his later years he lived at Alameda, New Mexico, where he died in 1940. Before his death he collaborated on an autobiography with Neil M. Clark, *Pardner of the Wind,* published in 1945.

The most definitive edition of Thorp's work is *Songs of the Cowboys, With Variants, Commentary, Notes, and Lexicon,* the latter material added by Austin E. and Alta S. Fife of Logan, Utah. Published by Clarkson N. Potter in 1966, this edition carried a complete facsimile of the Estancia pamphlet as well as musical scores and other material.

As far as is known, the Estancia printshop never produced another pamphlet to equal Thorp's. Fife says that perhaps not more than twenty copies of the little red-covered first edition remain. I know of at least three in private collections. In 1968 the heirs of the last owner of the Estancia shop gave most of the machinery of the closed printshop to the Museum of New Mexico. I went with the museum staff to select the most important pieces. One was an old platen press originally operated by a foot pedal, and this is now at the Museum. It could well be the press on which the first cowboy song book in America was printed.

ST. MICHAELS PRESS

The St. Michaels Press is unknown to most tourists who take Arizona state road 264 west through Window Rock, but the early books of this press are known internationally to anthropologists and linguists.

In 1898 the Franciscan order established a mission at the place then known as Cienega, just west of Window Rock. One of the priests, Fr. Anselm Weber, was urged by the early ethnologist Washington Matthews to master the Navajo language.

Two years later Fr. Anselm was joined by a remarkably capable helper, Fr. Berard Haile, who would spend a half century studying Navajo customs. He was born at Canton, Ohio, in 1874 and ordained in 1898. After two years as an assistant parish priest at Peoria, Illinois, he went to St. Michaels.

Working jointly with Fr. Anselm and Fr. Leopold Osterman, Fr. Berard drafted an ethnologic dictionary. This required an alphabet with variant characters to indicate certain sounds and inflections in Navajo speech.

During the early years the friars were encouraged by visiting ethnologists, including Stewart Culin who came out from the Brooklyn

Institute Museum in 1902. In 1908 Culin helped the priests acquire a large Chandler & Price platen press, operated at first by a treadle, later by a gasoline engine and eventually by electricity. Type was hand-set. The equipment was set up in a storage building about twenty feet square, built of squared logs, with a pyramid roof.

Fr. Berard began the formidable task of hand-setting and printing the 536 pages of *An Ethnological Dictionary of the Navaho Language* in an edition of two hundred copies. In this work he was aided by George Connolly, a Cincinnati printer who had come west for his health. Funds for materials and Connolly's labor were borrowed and supplemented by donations.

The book appeared in 1910. The press also issued in that year a *Navaho-English Catechism of Christian Doctrine,* subsidized by Mother Katharine Drexel, who also financed the building of St. Catherine Indian School in Santa Fe before she became a nun.

The dictionary is the first and most-sought item from the St. Michaels Press. A facsimile edition was done in Germany and another facsimile was recently done at St. Michaels.

After these first two books the press went into a decline for several years. The salary of $80 a month for printer Connolly was out of the question. The next few books were done by outside printers, and during the years 1915-1924

69

Fr. Berard was assigned to branch missions elsewhere on the Navajo reservation. In 1926 the press began its second era. Better equipment was secured, eventually including a Monotype keyboard and caster and a flatbed press. The staff grew to include Navajos trained in printing. By 1957 about twenty significant books had been published, all dealing with the rituals, language and ceremonials of the Navajo. A close examination of any copy will usually indicate whether it was done partly or wholly at the press or by an outside printer. The equipment is still in use, but the emphasis is no longer on scholarly works for a small audience. In 1954 Fr. Berard suffered a stroke and was sent to a hospital in Santa Fe, where he died in 1961.

WRITERS' EDITIONS

The 1920s saw a migration of writers to the Taos and Santa Fe areas, to which artists had already been attracted. This was also the decade in which beautiful limited editions were being produced all over the nation, and some of the Santa Fe writers yearned to see their works fittingly presented. But the start of the Great Depression in 1929, deepening within two years, discouraged most eastern publishers from venturing into editions that required extensive handwork and costly papers.

At that time Walter L. Goodwin, Jr., of an

old Main Line family near Philadelphia, was production manager and book designer for the J. B. Lippincott Company. He noticed that a group of people at Viking Press in New York City had established an after-hours cooperative to publish small books in beautiful formats. Their success, more in satisfaction than in cash, encouraged Goodwin and others to publish a series known as Arrow Editions. Goodwin had his own private press equipment, including fonts of Kennerley, Kabel and Caslon type, and he handled the group's production.

Out in Santa Fe two people who knew of Arrow Editions were Alice Corbin (Henderson), co-founder of *Poetry, A Magazine of Verse,* and the poet Haniel Long, a former professor of English at Harvard and Carnegie Tech, who had moved to Santa Fe in 1929. In 1932 they urged Goodwin to come to the Santa Fe area and bring his equipment.

Goodwin gave Lippincott a year's notice and arrived in New Mexico in the summer of 1933. He brought with him an ATF Kelly press, style B, and installed it in what had once been the dining hall of a health ranch for tuberculars at Tesuque just north of Santa Fe.

The Writers' Editions group began a serious effort, with Alice Corbin and Haniel Long leading the way. Peggy Pond Church was active in the group, as was Raymond Otis. Otis, who settled in Santa Fe in 1928, is perhaps best known for his novel, *Miguel of the Bright Mountain*.

By the end of 1933 the group had published its first three books. In order of appearance they were Alice Corbin's *The Sun Turns West*, Peggy Pond Church's *Foretaste* and Haniel Long's *Atlantides*.

The work was truly cooperative, following a philosophy described by Long in an essay in 1938 in *The Colophon, An Annual of Bookmaking*. Starting with five associates in 1933, the group had seventeen members by 1938. Each author underwrote the cost of printing his or her own work, at times helping to support a work by another. Part of the receipts went into a common fund. Each author was required to turn in a mailing list of prospective book buyers. All gathered to send out announcements or to wrap and ship a new book. Otis, who was a member but never published through Writers' Editions, served as financial secretary to keep members' accounts straight. By 1938 there were thirteen books bearing the Writers' Editions imprint.

It is important to keep in mind that the Writers' Editions and Rydal Press were separate entities. The Rydal Press served Writers' Editions as a production facility but also printed for others, such as completing several Arrow Editions books still in progress when Goodwin moved to New Mexico. Also, the Rydal Press did commercial work and published books bearing its own name.

The group soon learned that books could not always be printed from hand-set type because of the high cost. Rydal Press then installed a Monotype keyboard and caster and imported from England fonts of matrices for Eric Gill's beautiful Perpetua type face, the first brought to the United States. The Kelly cylinder press continued as the large press, but in 1934 Rydal acquired a 10 by 15 inch Colt's Armory platen press that had been used in San Francisco by Helen and Bruce Gentry. This press, ideal for small book work, was of a kind that had also been a favorite of the Grabhorns in San Francisco and Saul Marks in Los Angeles. In 1934 Bruce Gentry came from San Francisco to join Rydal as a designer and craftsman. He stayed until 1937 and then left to continue his career in the east. Bruce was most proud of his design for Haniel Long's *Interlinear to Cabeza de Vaca,* published as a Writers' Editions book in 1936.

Rydal Press remained in Tesuque about four years. In the summer of 1937 it moved to 998 Canyon Road in Santa Fe, to the building recently occupied by Jan Nelson's bookshop. By late 1941 Goodwin sold out his interest in Rydal Press, returned to the east for some years, and then lived a while in Arizona before returning to his ranch near Pojoaque, New Mexico. The press and building were sold to Dale Bullock and Gordon Stevenson. It continued for more than thirty years, doing commericial printing and also producing many books.

The Writers' Editions group continued until shortly before World War II, when its members scattered or became involved in other interests. The last book to bear the imprint probably was Gustave Baumann's *Frijoles Canyon Pictographs,* done in 1939-40. The typography was by Willard F. Clark, with part of the woodcuts by Baumann printed on his own handpress and the rest of the printing done in Clark's plant. The binding was by Hazel Dreis, a nationally recognized hand binder then living in Santa Fe.

Apparently no complete checklist exists of Writers' Editions books. Aided by Walter L. Goodwin, Jr., we submit the following list of seventeen, the only titles known to bear that imprint, arranged alphabetically by author:

Baumann, Gustave, *Frijoles Canyon Pictographs* (1939-40); Chávez, Fray Angélico, *Clothed With the Sun* (1939); Church, Peggy Pond, *Familiar Journey* (1936) and *Foretaste* (1933); Corbin, Alice, *A Child's Bouquet: Fifteen Songs for Children* (1935) and *The Sun Turns West* (1933); Davey, William, *Arms, Angels, Epitaphs & Bones* (1935); Fechin, Alexandra, *March of the Past* (1937); Fletcher, John Gould, *XXIV Elegies*

(1935); Johnson, Spud, *Horizontal Yellow* (1935); Long, Haniel, *Atlantides* (1933), *Interlinear to Cabeza de Vaca* (1936), *Malinche* (1939), *Pittsburgh Memoranda* (1935), and *Walt Whitman and the Springs of Courage* (1938); Rhodes, Eugene Manlove, *Penalosa* (1934); and Storm, Marion, *The Life of Saint Rose: First American Saint and the Only American Woman Saint* (1937).

If any others were done by the group, this would have to be confirmed by the authors or their records. The Haniel Long papers are in the University of California at Los Angeles Library; Alice Corbin Henderson's papers are in the possession of her daughter, Mrs. Edgar Rossin.

John Gould Fletcher's book was one of the nation's "Fifty Books" in 1936. Baumann's book made that pantheon in 1941. Consistently fine printing finally had arrived in New Mexico.

ALAN SWALLOW

Publisher-printer Alan Swallow has been identified most frequently with the city of Denver, but he did some of his formative work in Albuquerque from 1940 to 1942. His story, already well told in journals, needs a summary here because perhaps no other publisher in the Rocky Mountain West had such an impact on fine literature of the region in the first half of the twentieth century.

Raised on a Wyoming farm, Swallow began writing poetry in high school. He avidly bought stacks of the Haldeman-Julius Little Blue Books that sold for a nickel or dime. While an undergraduate at the University of Wyoming he launched a short-lived mimeographed literary magazine, *Sage*. He went on to Louisiana State University, 1937-40, to earn a doctorate with emphasis on literature.

While at LSU he borrowed $100 and bought a tabletop Kelsey press that could print a five by eight inch page. His first production was a set of two volumes in paper covers, *Signets, An Anthology of Beginnings*, by Brantley and Shorey, completed in March 1940. The next month he did his second work, *First Manifesto*, a pamphlet by Thomas McGrath.

Back in Wyoming during the summer of 1940, Alan Swallow began hand-setting his first full volume of poetry, *In Plato's Garden*, by Lincoln Fitzell. In the fall of that year he went to teach at the University of New Mexico in Albuquerque and there completed the book. He wrote later that he considered this his first trade book. It was bound by Hazel Dreis.

In Albuquerque he met Horace Critchlow, a graduate student at UNM, and they formed a partnership. They bought a 10 by 15 inch Chandler & Price press and installed the equipment in a rented garage. To meet expenses they did small printing jobs under the name of Big Mountain Press, often using Linotype slugs set in a Baptist printing house. For their own productions they used the imprint of Sage Books. Two of their most notable early books were *Three Spanish-American Poets*, a translation, and *Rocky Mountain Stories*, edited by Ray B. West. The first was issued only as a paperback, the second in both hardcover and paperback editions.

In 1942 Critchlow was drafted into military service. The partnership was dissolved amicably. Critchlow took the big press and Swallow went back to the little Kelsey. From 1943 until 1945 Swallow also was in military service.

After the war Swallow joined the faculty of Denver University but continued his own publishing. By 1954 publishing had become a full-time job, and he soon had a list of important authors including Frank Waters, Frederick Manfred, Vardis Fisher and Yvor Winters. Swallow was fifty-one when he died in 1966. The press's inventory, name and other rights were taken over by a group who moved the venture to Chicago and continued under the name of Swallow Press. The imprint is now at Ohio University Press.

CARL HERTZOG

In the typographic history of the Plains, the Rockies and the desert, the outstanding designer-printer unquestionably is Carl Hertzog of El

77

Paso. He has encouraged more bookworkers to do better work and has elevated the art of the book to a higher level than did any other person between the east coast and the Pacific shore. And he is a match for the best on either coast.

Carl lived in New Mexico for about two years as a small child. He had been born at Lyons, France, where his father, a musician, was on tour. Carl grew up in Pittsburgh where, at the age of ten he had a toy press, was a journeyman typesetter by the time he left high school, and studied for a while under Porter Garnett at the fabulous Laboratory Press at the Carnegie Institute of Technology.

He next took a job in West Virginia but left it to come to El Paso in 1923 when he was 21, answering a help-wanted advertisement of the McMath Company, printers. There he supervised his first book, *La Lepra Nacional,* by Gonzalo de la Parra, done for a Mexican customer in 1923. Carl worked for others until he opened his own shop in 1934. He later was a partner in the Guynes Printing Company, 1944-47, and from 1948 until his retirement, he was printer-in-residence and lecturer at what is today the University of Texas at El Paso.

At UTEP his first book from Texas Western Press was *The Spanish Heritage of the Southwest* (1952). Between 1923 and 1952 he did dozens of books, pamphlets and keepsakes.

78

In the fall of 1951 I had just moved from California to Houston and Carl came to pay a visit. "Let's talk printing," he opened, and started telling me how he had designed the edition of Ross Calvin's *River of the Sun,* published by UNM Press in 1946. For that book he was inspired by colors and motifs from prehistoric pottery.

In the years that followed we visited back and forth: when I went to El Paso or when he came to my Stagecoach Press in Santa Fe, or whenever our trails crossed at bookmen's meetings in the old Driskill Hotel in Austin, at Ted DeGrazia's hacienda in Tucson or over *chiles rellenos* in Juarez.

What ineffable secret made Carl Hertzog such a remarkable typographer? Commercial ink-slingers grumbled that he was a crazy perfectionist, but even while they spoke they tried to make their current job look a little less like something printed on a hay press with apple butter for ink. That, if anything, was Carl's real secret: the idea that you can do better if you try and still better if you try harder another time around. Add to this a serious study of the traditions of the great printers of the past, plus a love for your own craft, and each new book becomes a pleasurable challenge and not a breadwinning chore.

Once Hertzog showed me nearly sixty variant trial impressions of a line portrait Tom Lea had done for *The King Ranch* on which Carl was working in 1952. Carl experimented with different inks, different makeready and variations in textures. Tom did the drawing again, with slight changes. An ordinary printer would have been satisfied with the first attempt. The difference between any two adjacent proofs was slight but noticeable; the difference between the first and the last was astounding. Every serious printer who encountered Carl's work came away with the feeling that anyone could try harder. Today there are book designers all across the Southwest who readily admit their obligation to Hertzog's work.

Collectors also saw the quality of his work. He once told me that whenever one of his books appeared it was assured of an immediate sale of three hundred copies to collectors, who knew his printer's mark of a tall thin H crossed with a smaller C. Carl has retired, and his papers are at the library of UTEP. The library of Eastern New Mexico University in Portales has a fine collection of his books.

Many books printed or designed by Carl Hertzog are New Mexico items. A partial list includes *The Unpublished Letters of Adolphe F. Bandelier* (1942); *The Journey of Fray Marcos de Niza* (1949); *The Zia Company of Los Alamos* (1950); *Tales of the Tularosa* (1953); *Early Days in the Mogollons* (1958); *The Roots of Regional*

 80

Literature, by Lawrence Clark Powell (1959); *Arrott's Brief History of Fort Union* (1962); and *Ranch on the Ruidoso* (1968).

These eight publishers and printers of the Southwest carried printing to higher levels, passing traditions and inspiration up the ladder of time, each to another. Padre Martínez and his little textbooks at Taos, the Reverend Menaul at Laguna Pueblo, and Father Berard at the Arizona mission, Frank Holme whittling his woodblocks in a chickenhouse at Phoenix, and Jack Thorp pencilling his cowboy songs beside a roundup fire, each left an impress on his time, and it remains today. The Writers' Editions, Alan Swallow and Carl Hertzog took up their predecessors' composing sticks and put more than mere words into each line of hand-set letters. We are all better because they passed this way.

HOW COLLECTORS GET
THAT WAY

Clinton P. Anderson

WHEN I WAS a young newspaper man I always wondered how a collector got that way. I never thought that I would fall into that category.

At that time I had not discovered a rule which I later found in Muir who said, "No self-respecting collector of books needs a reason for collecting, he collects because he likes books." For years I went around accumulating books because I liked them. I was particularly interested in poetry and on frequent trips to New York I would go into the secondhand bookstores and buy as many books of poetry as I could afford, striving always for quantity and never worrying about editions or the condition of a particular volume.

One day I learned that a library which had belonged to a preacher was to be sold. The preacher had inherited it from a grandfather who had been a noted minister in his day. The books were to be sold in boxes, unopened, sight unseen. I bought them and paid nearly as much for the transfer company to bring them to my home and put them on a back sleeping porch as I did for the half dozen large boxes that contained the library.

When I opened the boxes, I sorted the books into subjects. Nearly everything related to theology. It was perhaps the thinnest harvest that a book collector ever realized. From it I kept the Harvard Classics and a dictionary. All the rest—nearly 2,000 books—I paid the transfer company to haul to the public library which, in turn, consigned the collection to a basement room on the odd chance that some student of theology might want a stray volume.

I had learned my first lesson: I would see what I bought thereafter.

In 1935 I was working for Harry Hopkins in the relief administration. Headquarters were in Salt Lake City, but much of my time had to be spent at San Francisco. We were handling states of huge area, and the relief problems in places like Los Angeles were extremely troublesome. By noon my nerves would stand no more of it for a while and, rather than have lunch in my office or at a hotel, I took to walking as far as I could away from the office. When I had worn myself out by rapid striding I would stop for a light lunch and then stroll leisurely back to the office. In that way my hour or hour and a half would bring new strength for the balance of the day.

I began to notice bookstores on my rambles. One day I determined to drop into one. It happened to be a store that specialized in Western Americana. The salesman asked me where my home was and when I told him it was New Mexico, he led me to a case with only New Mexico titles.

"These," he said softly, "are the standard items. I suppose you have all of these but if you'd give us a list of your wants, we would search for them and try to supplement what you now have."

The standard items! I did not own a single book in that entire case. I had lived in New Mexico for nearly 20 years and while I knew the poets who had centered largely around Santa Fe (I had shown some of my own verses to Alice Corbin and had admired—from a distance—Witter Bynner) I was wholly unacquainted with Coronado and the early explorers and had not even a slight acquaintance with Emory, Abert, Fremont, Edwards, Doniphan, Cooke and their great company.

I think it was the worst noon that I ever experienced. I couldn't imagine what I had been doing with my life. I wondered what I wanted with James Thomson's "The Seasons" or with the Oxford anthologies. Here were the

84

people who had influenced the life of my state and who had left their marks all over its face.

The next noon I was back with a note pad. I put down the price of every volume he had in that case and totalled it up to estimate how long it would take me to get "just the standard items." It came to about $2,000. My initial purchase was $200, but I was on my way.

From that time on for a dozen years it was the same story from daylight to dark. Every time I was footloose in a large city I went to the bookstores. Every evening after I had finished the daily paper I picked up the book catalogs. When I would go back to San Francisco I would drop by that store to make sure that I had in my library everything in my field that the store carried. But the field expanded. It seemed apparent that if I wanted to know much about the early conquistadores I would have to understand a lot about the Indians, so I sought Indian classics and studied the archeology of our Southwest. Then I branched off into mining and the stories of the cattle trail. I got interested in the history of cattle brands.

My attention was repeatedly called to stories of existing libraries filled with choice volumes, and I searched them out. One day a man told me of an attic in which there were 2,000 volumes which had not been looked at for 50 years. Within a few minutes I had driven to my home, picked up a suitcase and was on my way. Coveralls were a part of my standard equipment in my car, not because I anticipated car trouble but because I wore them as I plowed through the bookstores. After a few hours' drive I reached the town where the supposed library was housed but I got there in the evening and the owners of the home explained to me that the attic was unlighted. I offered to use a flashlight from my car but was told to be back in the morning.

If that first noon in San Francisco was a bad hour, that night of waiting to see the library untouched for 50 years was the worst I ever spent. The next morning I was there. Three hours of plowing through dust brought me the bad news that the 2,000 volumes consisted of the printed reports of Masonic Grand Lodges over the United States and there wasn't a single book in the entire collection that dealt with the history of New Mexico and not a single story of the cattle trail.

As I stood in the owner's kitchen, washing up and explaining to him my interests, he told me that I should have gone to a completely different part of the state where he knew a fine library existed and that it was exactly my field. The sleeplessness of the past night was forgotten. I could barely gulp down a light lunch and be on the road again. It was evening before I reached my destination but again at early morning I was where the books were supposed to be.

They weren't there. The Huntington Library had bought them ten years before. There were only a few fragments, some of them interesting. One, in particular, was a thick volume bound in sheepskin containing the ordinances and decrees of the consultation, provisional government of Texas and the convention which assembled at Washington, Texas, March 1, 1836, Houston 1838, and bound with that the laws of the Republic of Texas in two volumes, Houston 1838, plus laws of the Republic of Texas, Volume 3, Houston 1838, and the laws passed in the first session of the Third Congress in 1839, containing as well the index which Sabin (No. 94999) found in a few copies. After I got the volume home I read one of Eberstadt's catalogs which referred to my find and said "the present is one of four known copies." You will excuse me, Mr. Eberstadt, one of five!

The search goes on forever. This fall when I was ill at Albuquerque, I tried to locate a library which I had learned of ten years ago. It is presently misplaced but given time and a little health, I know I will find it. That is the hope that carries us all from one fruitless search to the next.

One day I was told that the library of

87

Mark Twain was in New Mexico in a little mining camp. I was on the road before 6 o'clock in the morning. When I reached the little town, not a soul seemed to know anything about Mark Twain except that he had written a book or two but had no relatives that anyone had ever heard about. I decided to try another course. I began to try to find out something about Samuel Clemens. Finally I found an old-timer who said, "Oh, no, you have his first name wrong. It wasn't Samuel. I forgot his name. He lived just a few houses down this road."

"Did he have books?" I asked.

The old miner broke into a hearty laugh. "Books, I should say he had. The house was full of them. He had them all around one room and halfway around another. He had them on the stairway going up to a little attic. The attic was full of them."

My pulse was a little more rapid but I tried to stay calm and not give myself away. "Where did he get them?"

"The family had them a long time," said my informant. "His grandfather was a great man, a great preacher, and he collected old religious manuscripts and books and the earliest examples of New England Bibles."

Maybe a Bay Psalm Book! My next question was as to the identity of the grandfather.

"I don't rightly know. Seems like his name

was maybe Jonathan Edwards. The old fellow used to talk about his grandfather. He had books that he said were scarce as hen's teeth. He had books. . ."

I stopped him. After all, there's a limit to what one collector can stand in a single morning.

"Where are his books? I'd like to see them."

"Well, I don't blame you. When he died he left half of them to the New Mexico State School of Mines and half to a priest who was living here. The priest took the old religious books, the very oldest ones. The others went to the School of Mines."

I was in my car on my way to the School of Mines in a very few minutes. The library had never been unboxed. It had been put away for future examination and indexing. A fire swept through the Administration Building of the School of Mines only a year or two before and had burned everything, books included. I was *that* close!

But we go right along. When I was the director of the United States Coronado Commission I sent a scholar to search through the Vatican library for the lost manuscripts of Bandelier. He had done a great story of the Indians and all scholars have found of it are the hand-illuminated chapter headings. The manuscript was done in Latin and presented by Bandelier to the Pope. It must be there somewhere.

That is how collectors get that way—"to strive, to seek, to find, and not to yield." Of course, more recently I have spent my time collecting items dealing with Franklin Roosevelt, but that's another story. I came to Washington as a member of the House of Representatives in the election which made Franklin Roosevelt the first third-term president in the history of this country. I concluded that regardless of partisanship the day would come when people would be interested in him. He had broken a great American tradition. He was to become our leader in a tremendous world war. His place in history was certain to be a large one. I asked myself what it would have been like to have been a congressman in Washington when Lincoln was president and to have had the hobby of book collecting. Such a person with a very little outside effort could have put together a priceless collection which his children or his children's children could have sold for a king's ransom when history had made a more accurate evaluation of one of the great men in American life.

Who knows what the place of Franklin Roosevelt will finally be? That's why I began to collect him. It's been great fun. So I close as I began—I need no reason for collecting; I just like books.

This piece first appeared in the 1952 edition of the

AB Bookman's Yearbook and is used with the kind permission of Mr. Jacob Chernofsky, editor of the *AB Bookman's Weekly*. Clinton Anderson was a dedicated bibliophile and his collection, left to the University of New Mexico General Library, became the cornerstone of their Southwestern Book Room. Born in South Dakota, he moved to Albuquerque in 1919 as a reporter and later editor for the Albuquerque *Journal*. In 1925 he became owner and operator of a general insurance agency in Albuquerque which still bears his name. His political career began in 1933 when he was appointed treasurer of the State of New Mexico. He then served in Congress as representative and in 1945 was appointed Secretary of Agriculture by President Truman. He resigned that post in 1948 to run successfully for the U. S. Senate, a post in which he served successive terms until illness forced his retirement. Anderson died in November 1975.

MY LOVE OF BOOKS
BEGAN EARLY

William A. Keleher

IN INTERVIEWING people who traveled in
and out of Albuquerque, I asked some of
them to give me the name of the book that had
been important in their lives. In some instances,
after interviewing people, I asked them to recommend a book for me to read, preferably one
that had been influential in their life work, and
if at all possible I read the recommended book.
I particularly recall that one man recommended
the *Memoirs of U. S. Grant* and I not only
read the *Memoirs,* in a two-volume edition, but
went on and plowed through the ten volumes
of Hay and Nicolay's *Life of Lincoln.* One man
told me to read Dumas. Professor J. C. Mon-
aghan of Notre Dame University did not recommend any particular book, but advised me
to "Read, read, read, write, write, write, speak,
speak, speak," if my goal was to be better educated. One man advised me to read Carlyle's
French Revolution, a two-volume work, which I
bought but never read beyond the first chapters.
My father and mother were both readers,

and I probably accrued a desire for reading from them. I recall that mother started me on the road to being a reader by giving me first *Robinson Crusoe,* and later the *Swiss Family Robinson.* For birthdays and Christmas gifts mother gave me books about George Washington, Patrick Henry, Robert E. Lee and other nationally known patriots. A persuasive and persistent book salesman sold mother a "complete set" of the novels of Charles Reade on the installment plan, three dollars down and fifty cents a week "until fully paid for." Mother allowed me to read all of Reade's novels with the exception of *Hard Cash* which she thought "too old" for me. Between ten and twelve years of age, I read all of the Reade novels, excepting the one forbidden. To this day I have never read *Hard Cash.* The Reade novels, among them *The Cloister and the Hearth,* '*Tis Never Too Late to Mend, A Terrible Temptation, Put Yourself in His Place,* and others to me then all absorbing stories, had no particular influence on my life insofar as I can recall. My father's favorite author was Charles Dickens and *David Copperfield* his favorite Dickens novel.

With an inclination to read in boyhood, and with newspaper reporting in more mature years, followed by legal training and work as a lawyer, it was perhaps only natural that the time would come when I would have the urge to write.

On July 5, 1929, at the Forty-eighth Annual Session of the Texas Bar Association, held in Amarillo, Texas, I read a paper on "Law of the New Mexico Land Grant," which marked the beginning of my venture into the field of regional historical writing. The New Mexico Bar Association had been invited to the Amarillo meeting as guests of the Texas Bar Association, and many New Mexico attorneys attended the sessions. My paper was published in the October 1929 issue of the *Texas Law Review*, on pages 154 to 170. As an indication of appreciation and friendship toward the New Mexico lawyers, the Association voted me an honorary life membership.

In preparing my paper, I had made a study of New Mexico land grants as they had existed under Spanish and Mexican rule and found that there was a human interest story connected with nearly every grant. I was interested in the extraordinary story of the Peralta-Reavis Grant and began serious study of its ramifications. I examined the files and stacks of papers, documents and transcripts of testimony in this case, contained in several filing cabinets then stored in Santa Fe in the Surveyor General's office, which were later transferred to the Bureau of Land Management office. After working on the Peralta-Reavis case for some months and writing several thousands of words on it, I decided to abandon the task, having reached the conclusion that the Peralta-Reavis story would not be of particular interest to the people of New Mexico.

The pleadings and proofs in the case, submitted to the Court of Private Land Claims, demonstrated beyond doubt that the alleged Grant, which measured fifty miles in width for hundreds of miles between Phoenix, Arizona, and Tierra Amarilla in Rio Arriba County, New Mexico, had been an attempted fraud of great magnitude. The evidence showed conclusively that one man, James Addison Peralta Reavis, was apparently a scoundrel, a master forger and a swindler. However, Reavis seemed to me to be a character who could not be successfully portrayed as in any way attractive or interesting. The evidence in the case proved that Reavis was an aggressive, indefatigable worker, persistent and persevering, possessing iron nerve, a man apparently without a single observable redeeming trait that I could discover. Having reached the conclusion that I should look further, I stopped work on James Addison Peralta Reavis and the Peralta-Reavis Grant and devoted effort to the history of the Maxwell Land Grant. I have never regretted that decision.

This piece is an excerpt from *Memoirs: 1892-1969, A New Mexico Item*, by William A. Keleher, published by

The Rydal Press, Santa Fe, in 1969. It is used with the kind permission of Loretta B. Keleher, wife of this highly acclaimed author of such works as *Maxwell Land Grant* (1942), *The Fabulous Frontier* (1945), *Turmoil in New Mexico: 1846-1868* (1952), and *Violence in Lincoln County: 1869-1881* (1957).

LAWRENCE CLARK POWELL
—BOOKMAN

Saul Cohen

LAWRENCE CLARK Powell, Larry to his friends, published an essay in 1941 called "John Fiske—Bookman." It is the title one feels compelled to use for a piece about him. (I'm not quite ready for "bookperson.") We who live in New Mexico are fortunate that his love of books is coupled with his love of the Southwest. Powell's fusion of life, landscape and literature in his writing about books and the Southwest has given us many hours of pleasure. For the majority of you who know his work, this is just a pleasant reminder. For the few of you who may not, it is an inadequate introduction.

A kind of fierce loyalty and enthusiasm are the hallmarks of those who know and love Powell's work, and he enjoys it. He is one of the great creative signers of his own books of our time. We were talking about my collection on Crete and he asked if I had Durrell's *The Dark Labyrinth*. I didn't think I did, but checked my shelves and sure enough there was the paperback.

[97]

On the cover was a quote from a book review in the New York *Times*. "That's a Powell item," he said, and proceeded to write inside the front cover, "Dear Saul. You have unwittingly collected an anonymous Powell item. The cover blurb is from my NYT review of the book. See how your investment has increased in value. Larry."

One reason he writes so well about the Southwest is that it is not his only interest. He has written about poets and poetry, history and travel, authors and printers. His latest work, to the extent one can keep track, appears to be his second novel, *The River Between* (Capra, 1979). His first novel, *The Blue Train* (Capra, 1977), written many years ago, may become a film.

But it always comes back to books. Powell once wrote: "Together with my home, bookshops and libraries have been the places on earth wherein I have spent the most time during the past quarter-century of my working life." Just as the twinkle in his eye never seems to stop, so his pen never seems to stop. He is perhaps the most prolific writer of forewords and introductions of our time. Sometimes the introduction is better than the book.

For someone who wants the full record, there's the *Checklist of the Published Writings of Lawrence Clark Powell*, compiled by Betty Rosenberg and published in 1966 by the UCLA libraries on the occasion of his retirement as Dean of the UCLA School of Library Science. A necessary supplement is the checklist from June 1966 to September 1976 by Robert Mitchell which appears in *Voices from the Southwest / A Gathering in Honor of Lawrence Clark Powell* (Northland, 1976), published on the occasion of his 70th birthday.

Apart from these, what are the essential volumes in a Powell collection? One should above all have the various collections of essays: *Islands of Books* (Ward Ritchie, 1951); *Books West Southwest: Essays on Writers, Their Books, and Their Land* (Ward Ritchie, 1957, repr. Greenwood, 1974); *A Passion for Books* (World, 1958, repr. Greenwood, 1974); *Books in My Baggage: Adventures in Reading and Collecting* (World, 1960, repr. Books for Libraries, 1971); *Bookman's Progress: The Selected Writings of Lawrence Clark Powell* (Ward Ritchie, 1968); and *From the Heartland* (Northland, 1976). Many of the essays were first published in periodicals or as separate pamphlets. Hardly anything of Powell's gets published only once.

Three essential bibliographical works are *Southwestern Book Trails: A Reader's Guide to the Heartland of New Mexico and Arizona* (Horn and Wallace, 1963); *Heart of the Southwest: A Selective Bibliography of Novels, Stories and Tales Laid in Arizona and New Mexico & Adjacent*

Lands (Dawsons, 1955, reprinted in *Arizona Highways,* Feb. 1957); and *A Southwestern Century: A Bibliography of One Hundred Books on Non-fiction about the Southwest* (J. E. Reynolds, 1958, reprinted in *Arizona Highways,* March 1958).

Basic also are the two volumes of essays on California and Southwestern authors originally published in *Westways* magazine and reprinted by Ward Ritchie: *California Classics* (1971) and *Southwest Classics* (1974). Then of course there is the autobiography, *Fortune and Friendship* (Bowker, 1968); *Arizona: A Bicentennial History* (Norton, 1976); *Photographs of the Southwest* (Ansel Adams photographs with an essay on the land by Lawrence Clark Powell; New York Graphic Society, 1976), and much, much more. I find only one grievous lack in Powell's writings. He hasn't written anything about Sherlock Holmes.

Saul Cohen is a practicing attorney in Santa Fe. He has written numerous articles on the Southwestern book world for *New Mexico Magazine* and *Book Talk* and is author of the book, *Author's Guide to Scholarly Publishing and the Law.* He is a longtime personal friend of Lawrence Clark Powell.

AN ARIZONA READING LIST

Lawrence Clark Powell

OF THE COMPILING of bibliographies and reading lists there is happily no end. I have been doing it for years—in *Westways, Books of the Southwest, Arizona Highways* and *New Mexico Magazine,* and in such books as *Libros Californianos, California Classics* and *Southwest Classics.* Readability, accuracy and availability rather than rarity and academic scholarship were my criteria, nor did I seek to be comprehensive and exhaustive. Yet to be undertaken is the compilation of an inclusive bibliography of Arizona, admittedly a formidable task.

When in 1976 I wrote on Arizona in the American Association of State and Local History's series The States and the Nation, published by W. W. Norton Co., I followed the series pattern and included "Suggestions for Further Reading." I am glad of this opportunity offered by *Book Talk* to edit the list as well as to add a few titles published in the past four years.

My prejudices and limitations, not to ignore my ignorance, are apparent in my choices and failures to choose. The classic clichés don't interest me. Frontier violence, ghost towns, lost mines, cowboy-Indian stuff, I leave to others. Mine is merely one reader's view of his adopted state. Other readers, other choices.

Not all the books listed are in print. Older works will be found in libraries and secondhand bookstores. Publishing on Arizona flourishes in Flagstaff at Northland Press, in Tempe at the Arizona Historical Foundation and in Tucson at the Arizona Historical Society and the University of Arizona Press. The Rio Grande Press in New Mexico has reprinted many of the classic works on the Southwest.

There are two good historical quarterlies: *Arizona and the West* (University of Arizona Press), and *Journal of Arizona History* (Arizona Historical Society). *Books of the Southwest,* edited by David Laird, is a monthly listing of current Southwest Americana published by the University of Arizona Library. *Arizona Highways* is more than a glamorous monthly of color photographs. Its articles are a valuable source of local history and folklore, arts and crafts and urban growth. Needed is a good index to the rich backfiles. In 1979 the magazine published a boxed set of six illustrated books by various writers on the state's heritage, Indians, wildlife, upland, canyons and deserts.

Although the political boundaries of Arizona

separate it precisely from its neighbors, the Southwest—of which Arizona and New Mexico are the heartland—is bounded more subtly by geography and weather and the imprint of its original possessors. And so the list begins with a book that describes the Southwest in terms of the land and the movement of its peoples.

D. W. Meinig, *Southwest* (Oxford, 1971). This 151 page book, subtitled "Three Peoples in Geographical Change, 1600-1970," is a compact essay on the power of the land to determine history. Natt N. Dodge and Herbert S. Zim, *The American Southwest: A Guide to the Wide Open Spaces* (Simon and Schuster, 1955) is remarkable for the colored lithographs which illuminate the pages on geography, history, archaeology, fauna, flora and crafts. Erna Fergusson, *Our Southwest* (Alfred Knopf, 1940), though out of date on current things, remains the best cultural introduction to the Southwest. Howard R. Lamar, *The Far Southwest, 1846-1912: A Territorial History* (Yale, 1966; W. W. Norton, 1970) is an outstanding work by Yale's professor of western history and includes New Mexico, Colorado, Utah and Arizona.

Jay J. Wagoner, *Early Arizona: Prehistory to Civil War* (U. of Arizona, 1975) and *Arizona Territory, 1863-1912: A Political History* (U. of Arizona, 1970) are authoritative works by an Arizona historian and are to be followed by a

103

history of the state since its creation in 1912. Ross Santee, editor, *Arizona: A Guide to the Grand Canyon State* (Hastings House, 1940 and later revision) and the companion New Mexico guide are among the best of the WPA series that came from the Depression. The book is timelessly valuable for its history, folklore and travel itineraries. Except for the urban centers, most of Arizona remains unchanged. The reason Santee's name does not appear as editor is that the WPA officials refused to list the names of his staff. "OK," the tough wrangler said, "then leave mine out."

A useful work is Andrew Wallace's *Sources and Readings in Arizona History* (Tucson, 1965). Walker and Bufkin's *Historical Atlas of Arizona* (U. of Oklahoma, 1979) is an indispensable work. The Tucson Corral of The Westerners has published three Brand Books (1967-76) which are a rich mine of history and folklore of southern Arizona.

Members of the faculty of the University of Arizona produced the revised second edition of *Arizona: Its People and Resources* (U. of Arizona, 1960, 1972) which constitutes an encyclopedia of the history, land, government, economy and cultural institutions. Will C. Barnes, *Arizona Place Names* (U. of Arizona, 1935, 1960) is the book to travel with in its first edition. The enlargement by Byrd R. Granger in 1960 is a large volume arranged by county rather than alphabetically as is the earlier edition, thus making quick reference difficult. Odie B. Faulk, *Arizona: A Short History* (U. of Oklahoma, 1970) is a compact work by the Southwest's most prolific historian. Madeline F. Paré and Bert M. Fireman, *Arizona Pageant: A Short History of the 48th State* (Arizona Historical Foundation, 1970) was written as a text for Arizona high schools. Marshall Trimble, *Arizona: A Panoramic History of a Frontier State* (Doubleday, 1977) is good history in a highly readable form.

Edward H. Spicer, *Cycles of Conquest: The Impact of Spain, Mexico and the United States on the Indians of the Southwest, 1530-1960*, drawings by Hazel Fontana (U. of Arizona, 1962) is a massive work that will probably remain definitive until our culture is supplanted by others. Charles Polzer, S.J., *A Kino Guide* (Southwestern Mission Research Center, 1972) is a biography and guide to Kino's missions and monuments. It contains a chapter on the discovery in 1966 of his grave in Magdalena, Sonora. Cartography is by Don Bufkin. John L. Kessell, *Mission of Sorrows: Jesuit Guevavi and the Pimas, 1691-1767* (U. of Arizona, 1970) is sound history, well written. Herbert E. Bolton, editor and translator, *Anza's California Expeditions*, 5 volumes (repr. Russell & Russell, 1966), combines scholarship in archives and field with readability.

Elliott Coues, editor and translator, *On the Trail of a Spanish Pioneer: The Diary of Francis Garcés. . .1775-1776,* 2 volumes (F. P. Harper, 1900) ranks with the Bolton-Anza at the peak of Arizona historiography. Coues was an army doctor in the Southwest who trailed Garcés as Bolton did Anza. James Ohio Pattie, *Personal Narrative,* edited by M. M. Quaife (R. R. Donnelley, 1930) is a romantic yarn by an illiterate trapper, which in its first edition sells for thousands of dollars. This Lakeside Classics reprint is the handiest of several versions. Pattie came down the Gila in the 1820s. His garrulous narrative was written for him by Timothy Flint. William H. Emory, *Lieutenant Emory Reports: A Reprint of. . .Notes of a Military Reconnaissance,* abridged by Ross Calvin (U. of New Mexico, 1968) was penned by the topographical engineer Emory who accompanied Kearny on his dash to California with dragoons, mules and a brass howitzer. Emory's notes rank with Garcés' diary as prime Arizoniana.

J. Ross Browne, *Adventures in Apache Country,* edited by Donald M. Powell (U. of Arizona, 1974) is a facsimile reprint, with added material, of the original Harper edition of 1869. This is the best of all travel books on southern Arizona in the 1860s. Browne's prose and drawings are happily wed in a book humorous, sardonic and civilized. John G. Bourke, *On the*

106

Border With Crook (Charles Scribner's Sons, 1891, and a photographic paperback edition by the U. of Nebraska, 1971). Martha Summerhayes, *Vanished Arizona: Recollections of the Army Life of a New England Woman* (Arizona Silhouettes, 1960) was first published in 1908 by Lippincott and enlarged by the author in 1911 (Salem Press). This classic of the Apache frontier in the 1870s has often been reprinted. This edition, which reproduces the text of 1911, with added historical notes by Ray Brandes, is the best modern version, sharing this distinction with a U. of Nebraska reprint of the same 1911 edition (1979), with an introduction by Dan Thrapp.

Frank C. Lockwood, *Pioneer Portraits: Selected Vignettes*, Introduction by John Bret Harte (U. of Arizona, 1968) is drawn from the author's *Pioneer Days in Arizona* (1932). The author came to the University of Arizona as an English professor, fell in love with Arizona, and became one of its most humanistic historians and biographers. Robert L. Sharp, *Big Outfit: Ranching on the Baca Float* (U. of Arizona, 1974) is a book Frank Dobie would have loved. Charles S. Peterson, *Take Up Your Mission: Mormon Colonizing Along the Little Colorado River, 1870-1900* (U. of Arizona, 1973) is the best account of the Mormons' contribution to the civilizing of Arizona. Ira B. Joralemon, *Copper: The Encompassing Story of Mankind's First Metal*

(Howell-North, 1973) is an enlarged edition of the author's *Romantic Copper* (Appleton-Century, 1935). The Arizona story is a major part of this world-wide account. Frank Waters, *The Colorado* (Rinehart & Co., 1946) is a volume in the Rivers of America series in which the author sought the mystical spirit of the river and the area it drains, as well as the geological and human history.

Bruce Babbitt, compiler, *Grand Canyon: An Anthology,* contains selections from Coronado to Zane Grey (Northland Press, 1979). Richard E. Lingenfelter, *Steamboats on the Colorado River* (U. of Arizona, 1978) is a chronicle of a vanished species, which is nearly true also of *Railroads of Arizona, Volume I: Southern Roads,* by David Myrick (Howell-North, 1975).

Frank McNitt, *The Indian Traders* (U. of Oklahoma, 1962) covers an important part of our history and has been solidly researched and engagingly written by a New England writer with a passion for the Southwest. Don Perceval and Clay Lockett, *A Navajo Sketch Book* (Northland Press, 1962) is a blend of drawings by Perceval and text by Lockett in this most beautiful of Arizona books. Clara Lee Tanner, *Southwest Indian Craft Arts* (U. of Arizona, 1968) is an authoritative work by an anthropologist and art historian and was supplemented by her later *Southwest Indian Painting: A Changing Art* (U.

of Arizona, 1973). Another valuable source is *Indians of Arizona: A Contemporary Perspective*, by various writers (U. of Arizona, 1974).

William T. Hornaday, *Camp-Fires on Desert and Lava* (Charles Scribner's Sons, 1908) gives account of an exploring trip by a party including a botanist, zoologist, geographer and sportsman to the little-known Pinacate volcanic desert, across the border southwest of Tucson. Edward Abbey, *Cactus Country* (Time-Life, 1973) is vintage Abbey, somewhat mellowed. Godfrey Sykes, *A Westerly Trend* (Arizona Pioneers Historical Society, 1944) is an autobiography of a hardy Yorkshireman who wandered west in the 1880s. Before he died in old age at Tucson, he became a cattleman, architect-engineer, hydrographer and explorer.

Ruth M. Underhill, *Singing for Power: The Song Magic of the Papago Indians of Southern Arizona* (U. of California, 1938; paperback reprint, Ballantine, 1973); the translation and commentary by the author and illustrations by Indian boys form a book of beauty and meaning.

John C. Van Dyke, *The Desert* (Charles Scribner's Sons, 1901), with many reprintings, was the first book to praise the southwestern desert as a place of beauty. It was written by an eastern art historian who "went native" for several years at the turn of the century and has been a book of lasting influence and authority

109

on the geology, fauna and flora, sky and weather of the Mojave, Colorado and Sonora deserts. In 1976 the Arizona Historical Society published a facsimile of the corrected second edition of 1902 with map by Don Bufkin and introduction by Lawrence Clark Powell.

Joseph Wood Krutch, *The Desert Year* (Viking Press, 1963) is available in later reprints of this work first published in 1951. After the distinguished literary figure came to Tucson in 1950 he distilled these essences from his first year of residency. His view of the arid land is that of a philosophical naturalist. This book complements Van Dyke's *The Desert* of a half century earlier. Lawrence Clark Powell, *Southwest Classics: The Creative Literature of the Arid Lands: Essays on Books and Their Writers* (Ward Ritchie Press, 1974) collects authors from Kino to Krutch and includes historians, naturalists, biographers and novelists.

Lawrence Clark Powell is the premier evangelist for books in the Southwest. His many careers have included bookseller, librarian, literary critic, historian and novelist. He lived for a time in Santa Fe, but has now settled in Tucson.

CONFESSIONS OF A NEW MEXICO BOOK REVIEWER

Alice Bullock

IF PUBLISHERS are the obstetricians who deliver an author's brain of its dreams, the nurses in attendance are the reviewers. A few are trained, but the vast majority are autodidacts with only one trait in common—a consuming desire to read. These reviewers would far rather read and review good books than bad ones, but they get all kinds. Some books rumble in like diesels and try to run you down by sheer weight. Others come in like sub-compacts with both doors open, flapping noisily. The reviewer tries to behave like a brave little traffic light and not turn yellow.

Many newspapers in New Mexico do not carry book reviews at all. Some feel that there is not enough reader interest or, if such were generated, that those readers would have no access to the books reviewed. Others feel that reviews are nothing but free advertising, which is at least partially true. Others have difficulty getting reviews of truly current books, since some slow and cautious reviewers may take as long as six or eight months to get a book read and the review written. Reviews should be published as close to the book's publication date as possible, and publishers do make an effort to place copies in the reviewers' hands two or three weeks in advance. If the book is reviewed eight months later, those few stores that had the book may already have given up on them and returned the title to the publisher's warehouse.

Space for reviews fluctuates and part of a reviewer's frustration is, though his copy is on time, advertising preempts the space, and no one on a newspaper fights an advertiser. Generally, our newspapers and magazines in New Mexico seldom receive an ad directly from a publisher. But some of our wider-awake booksellers advertise frequently.

A personal credo that has directed my reviewing efforts over the years here in New Mexico is to determine as rapidly as possible what the author is striving to accomplish. If he succeeds, then it is a good book. Many reviewers take delight in finding a soft spot on the underbelly of a book and tearing it to pieces. Much of this type of reviewing, so it seems from my perch on the corral post, is nothing more than ego pap. Such reviewers are anxious to show how smart they are rather than give enough about the book to enable the reader to decide whether or not it is a book he wants to buy or borrow from the library. Even worse is the reviewer who finds a few errors and dwells on them, ignoring the thousands of correct statements in the book. Sometimes of course I have to do an unfavorable review and it is then that I wish I could say, a la Ambrose Bierce, that the covers are too far apart—but he beat me to it!

Much of the lack of adequate book reviewing in New Mexico lies squarely on the shoulders of the people our newspapers and magazines serve. Editors do listen to their subscribers. If people would let editors know they read reviews, they would no doubt get more of them. A book reviewer with few editors interested in publishing his reviews sometimes feels as though he were playing tennis with a brick wall: lots of exercise, but no matches won!

Some local authors just can't write. A great deal of reading affords me no reason to doubt that. But then, after reading a book I loathed, I will run into someone who loved it. This in turn reminds me that we all have our mental blocks to play with. All the reviewer can do is put honest opinion on the line. He does not have to be right, but he does have to be as honest as possible. This can be very painful.

When a writer I know and like personally turns out a poor piece, I want to retreat inside my head and slam the door. But the review often has to be written, even though I feel like a celluloid cat being chased through hell by an asbestos dog. Being true to this reviewing craft, I write an honest review; and thereafter, like the gunman of the old west, I sit with my back to the wall waiting for the worst.

The real joy of the reviewer comes when the postman delivers a really good book. Then while dishes pile up in the kitchen and the ironing mildews, I read. My housewife eyes are kissed with the secret shame of dreams as I leave the shores of everyday to travel in a time that is permitted to remain absolute, not for the sake of truth, but for the sake of vicarious living.

A common comment to me is "I don't have time to read books, but reading your reviews keeps me posted on new Southwestern books." I would much rather they felt impelled to read the book, but I will settle for what I can get. But I do wish that instead of telling me, good or bad, they would write and tell my newspaper editor.

I truly like sharing my joy in reading. It has been said that most reviewers are frustrated writers. There is probably a lot of truth to that. But in defense of book reviewers, they are not *has-beens*, but are more likely *never-weres*, as far as published authors are concerned. The readers of reviews might do well to be as lenient with reviewers as the reviewers are with authors.

Oscar Wilde said that there was only one

114

thing in the world worse than being talked about: not being talked about. If your book got a review, be glad!

Alice Bullock came to New Mexico in 1912 at the age of eight, and New Mexico has not been the same since. Her unbounded curiosity is matched only by her energy. She has reviewed books for almost every major magazine, journal and newspaper in New Mexico, written books on the ghosts, villages and history of northern New Mexico, and taught school in communities that have long since become ghost towns. Alice and her husband, Dale Bullock, live in Santa Fe.

FROM THE PEN OF A REGIONAL
HISTORIAN

Father Stanley

ALTHOUGH A native of New York, I have now lived the greater part of my life in the Southwest, mostly in New Mexico and Texas. I truly consider myself a Southwesterner. Life has been inspiring in the Southwest—fresh air, kind people and a greatness that seems to latch on to all who come here. From the days of Oñate to the present, many men have felt this goodness that truly is the Southwest. It is a heritage and a trust. More and more visitors come to our area and, in the end, become a part of it. We can certainly understand how the Indians of the Southwest have loved this country for centuries.

When first arriving in New Mexico I noticed great interest in and fascination with the many stories about Billy the Kid, Clay Allison and others of their ilk. When someone pointed out a hole in a window made by a bullet intended for Jesse James (who never saw that town, much less ate in that café), I decided it was time to prove to people that the truth was as fascinating as fiction—particularly so in New Mexico.

My interest was not so much in personal publicity, as in New Mexico publicity. This is truly a land of enchantment, full of heritage which must be preserved. And this has been the general theme of each of my booklets and books on the glorious state. My efforts to chronicle many of the places of the past are for the purpose of preserving for the future such names as Blossburg, Alaska, Inez, Carbonateville, Bonanza City, which were all once part of the blood-stream of Territorial days, but are all too easily forgotten because no one took the time to see that New Mexicans yet unborn could read about them and the price their ancestors paid to give them a place in the sun. Dawson, Brilliant, Yankee—a litany of names as fascinating as the people who made them.

My writing has certainly not been acceptable to all. For every nice letter received there are ten disagreeing with the facts I have dug up. But crusaders should never look for more than the Cross anyway. And critics should never be one's "razor's edge." After all, God must love them—He made so many.

Francis L. Stanley Crocchiola is far better known to New Mexicans as F. Stanley, the compiler, writer, regional historian who produced over 150 books and pamphlets on the histories of the living and dead communities of New

117

Mexico and, more recently, of West Texas. F. Stanley was born in New York, educated at Catholic University, and sent to New Mexico by his superiors in the Church because of a lung condition. His physical misfortune became our fortune, because of the records of New Mexico he has preserved. Now retired, he lives in Nazareth, Texas.

IS THERE VALUE IN THAT
OLD BOOK?

Jack Potter & Nicholas Potter

UNFORTUNATELY for most treasure hunters, the majority of old books have no monetary value at all. More often than not, this is because the subject matter is no longer of interest to the buying public—and something is only worth what someone will pay for it. There is little demand for most old Bibles, bestselling fiction, textbooks, book club books, encyclopedias and dictionaries, religious tracts and sermons, and technical books that are out-of-date (i.e., more than a few years old). In fact many, possibly most, books that have value are not *old* but recent. There are more books published in the years 1930-1980 that still have some value than books published from 1880-1930.

Condition is of prime importance in determining the value of a book. Copies in fine condition are always worth more than copies in only fair or poor condition. Books that lack plates or with badly worn bindings are probably worthless. Very few books are worth rebinding, though skillful minor repair can at least make a book usable.

Certain books are obviously valuable. In an age of paperbacks a well-crafted older book will always attract attention. A sumptuous leather binding or excellent illustrations or finely printed pages on handmade paper will identify these books immediately as having some monetary value today. Many titles by well known modern authors have value, especially *literary* authors such as Mark Twain, Ernest Hemingway, William Faulkner, Henry James and so on. Such books have considerably more value if they are first editions (including signed, limited editions) or inscribed by the author.

Some sets of books have great value; most sets have none at all. Sets of the collected works of single authors, such as Melville, Twain, Hardy, Dickens, Conrad, James, Tolstoi, etc., are definitely sought after. Sets of encyclopedias, travel lectures, and old histories are generally without value, as are the Book of Knowledge, the Pageant of History and sets of regional fiction, such as Great French Novels.

Many history books are valuable—not general surveys but local histories or firsthand accounts of specific historical events. These are sometimes referred to as Americana. Similar monographs dealing with non-American history would have much less value, there being much less demand for them in this country. Art, music, philosophy, good poetry, the occult, some science (though science is a field that changes every day, and most scientific and technical books are out-of-date in a few years)—these are the fields, in addition to those already mentioned, in which there is steady interest on the part of a book-buying public.

If you have what you believe is a rare or valuable book, you can consult *American Book Prices Current* in your public library to see if a copy more or less like yours has sold at auction in recent years, the price it brought, etc. Neither the inclusion nor absence of your book from this source necessarily means that your copy is or is not of value, but it is a guideline. You should also check *Books in Print* at the library or local bookstore, to see if the specific edition you have is still in print and at what price.

You must be very careful in interpreting the data you find about a specific book in any guide to book prices. There are many changes taking place all the time. Prices given, even when they may be shown "$15-$35," can be misleading. You can no more accurately evaluate your particular book from such descriptions than you can diagnose your particular ailment from reading a medical book.

If a book is said to be worth $30, this usually refers to its value to the ultimate buyer. If a dealer is to sell the book for $30, he cannot buy it from you at that price. He cannot pay

$25 either, for his volume is not sufficiently high to allow him to work on the kind of markup a drug store can get by on. What he will pay for a $30 book will depend on how soon he thinks he can sell it, though if he cannot offer $12.50 to $15 he probably does not want it at all. It may be a good enough title, but not one for which he gets calls. But any good dealer in used and rare books will always be glad to look at any books you have for sale, and in consultation will share the information that only experience teaches.

Dealers do not make house calls except where a collection is involved, but they buy and sell all day long and will be glad to talk to you, look at your list of titles, and examine books you bring to their store or office.

There is no simple method of placing a specific value on a book. Book dealers with years of experience are learning their trade every day, just as a doctor or lawyer or mechanic or artist does. And there will always be mistakes in judgment as there are always new things to learn. But there is a definite book-buying market, and a dealer with experience and the proper reference library will always be able to give a qualified evaluation of your books.

If there is no used bookstore near you, write to the Antiquarian Booksellers Association of America, 50 Rockefeller Plaza, New York,

 122

New York 10020, and they will refer you to someone to whom you can then address an inquiry.

This piece, first written by Jack Potter in December 1974, just prior to his death, is presented here as revised by his son Nicholas. Jack Potter Bookseller, a long honored name in antiquarian books in Santa Fe, is now Nicholas Potter Bookseller. Nicholas has followed in his father's footsteps as the proprietor and as a member of the Antiquarian Booksellers Association of America.

A NEW MEXICO BOOK
COLLECTION

Jack D. Rittenhouse

IT IS NOT TOO difficult to compile a list of a hundred or so books that may be called a collector's collection of books about New Mexico. Each collector sets his or her own rules, but for this first list we might agree that we will list only books of several printed pages done in English. This rules out the rich Spanish period, handwritten diaries, single sheet handbills and maps.

There are two broad groups of books available: those printed by the government and those printed by publishing firms or individuals. The government published reports of exploring expeditions. A few of these appeared before the United States troops occupied New Mexico in 1846; in the early years, before government funds were available, books by such explorers as Zebulon Pike were issued by private firms.

Most government publications fall into the category of primary works. That is, they were first-hand observations; they say: I was there and this is what I saw. When another writer rewrites the story, working from primary accounts, his new book is a secondary account. All primary works are valuable, for they are source material. But this does not mean that secondary works are not valuable, for they provide interpretation and meaning and examine conflicting accounts in an effort to arrive at the truth.

Ten landmark items stand out among the government reports. As a 20-word title is not uncommon on a Congressional document, we will use here the shortened titles that are convenient handles among book people.

Abert, James W., *Report of Examination of New Mexico* (1848). Emory, William H., *Notes of a Military Reconnaissance* (1848). Emory, William H., *U. S. and Mexican Boundary Survey* (1857-58, 4 parts in 2 vols., but be happy if you get the first volume). Johnson, Joseph E., and others, *Routes from San Antonio to El Paso* (1850). McCall, George A., *Reports in Relation to New Mexico* (1851). Macomb, John N., *Expedition from Santa Fe to Grand and Green Rivers* (1876). *Pacific Railroad Surveys* (1855), especially the volumes with reports by Amiel Whipple, John Parke and John Pope. Simpson, James H., *Military Reconnaissance from Santa Fe to the Navajo Country* (1852). Wislizenus, Frederick A., *Memoir of a Tour to Northern Mexico* (1848).

All were issued by Congress, although some

125

were published before there was a central printing house in Washington. A really fine New Mexico collection will include other government reports, always known as "documents." A few of these are quite scarce. The 1818 document usually listed as *Imprisonment of Certain American Citizens at Santa Fe* is a triple-crowned item: first U. S. government document dealing solely with an event in New Mexico; with what became the Santa Fe Trail; and with the Southwestern fur trade. It fits in with four other government reports of that same general theme and period: *Answers of Augustus Storrs* (1825); Alphonso Wetmore's *Petition of Sundry Inhabitants of Missouri* (1825); Bennett Riley's *Protection of Trade Between Missouri and Mexico* (1830); and President Andrew Jackson's *Message on the Fur Trade and Inland Trade with Mexico* (1832).

Other significant documents of this early period are: Abert, James W., *Through the Country of the Camanche [sic] Indians* (1846). Beale, Edward F., *Wagon Road from Fort Defiance* (1858). Cooke, Philip St. George, *Journal: Santa Fe to San Diego* (1849). Graham, James D., *Boundary Line Between U. S. and Mexico* (1853). Michler, Nathaniel H., *Routes from Western Boundary of Arkansas to Santa Fe* (1850). Ruffner, Ernest H., *Lines of Communication Between Southern Colorado and Northern New Mexico* (1876). Simpson, James H., *Route *from Fort Smith to Santa Fe* (1850). Sitgreaves, Lorenzo, *Expedition Down the Zuni and Colorado Rivers* (1853).

Among the books by explorers and travelers published by commercial firms, here is a double dozen that belong in any collection on New Mexico:

Bartlett, John R., *Personal Narrative...With Mexican Boundary Commission* (N.Y., 1854). Cutts, James M., *Conquest of California and New Mexico* (Phila., 1847). Davis, William W. H., *El Gringo* (N. Y., 1857). Edwards, Frank S., *A Campaign in New Mexico* (Phila., 1847). Falconer, Thomas, *Notes of a Journey Through ...New Mexico* (London, 1844). Froebel, Julius, *Seven Years Travel in Central America... and Far West* (London, 1859). Hughes, John T., *Doniphan's Expedition* (Cincinnati, 1847). James, Thomas, *Three Years Among the Indians and Mexicans* (Waterloo, Ill., 1846). Kendall, George W., *Narrative of Texan Santa Fe Expedition* (N. Y., 1844). Mollhausen, Balduin, *Diary of a Journey From the Mississippi to...the Pacific* (London, 1858). Pattie, James Ohio, *Personal Narrative* (Cincinnati, 1831). Peters, DeWitt C., *Life and Adventures of Kit Carson* (N. Y., 1858). Pike, Albert, *Prose Sketches and Poems* (Boston, 1834). Reid, John C., *Reid's Tramp* (Selma, Ala., 1858). Richardson, William H., *Journal of...* (Baltimore, 1847). Rob-

127

inson, Jacob S., *Sketches of the Great West* (Portsmouth, N. H., 1848). Ruxton, George A. F., *Adventures in Mexico and the Rocky Mountains* (London, 1847), also his *Life in the Far West* (Edinburgh, 1849). Udell, John, *Journal of.* . . (Suisun City, Cal., 1859; get a reprint, for only two copies are known of the first printing). Wilson, Richard L., *Short Ravelings From a Long Yarn* (Chicago, 1847).

In this early period the work with the most far-reaching influence may have been Zebulon Pike's *An Account of Expeditions*. . . (Phila., 1810). Also influential was Josiah Gregg's *Commerce of the Prairies* (N. Y., 1844). Perhaps the most readable of all primary accounts is Lewis H. Garrard's *Wah-To-Yah and the Taos Trail* (Cincinnati, 1850). Two contemporary reports on the Civil War in New Mexico are Hollister, Ovando J., *History of the 1st Regiment of Colorado Volunteers* (Denver, 1863) and Noel, Theophilus, *A Campaign from Santa Fe to the Mississippi* (Shreveport, 1865, and quite rare).

This is not a complete list of all publications by early travelers but only those generally considered as the foundation of a collection. Many other first-hand works were written during the years 1810-76 but not published until years later.

In judging any early edition, make sure the maps are present. Several books were issued in paper covers or "wrappers." Other short government publications were issued in bound volumes containing several reports; these are often separated and the individual reports sold as "disbound" items, *i.e.*, without covers.

As a category the government documents are among the best buys on today's market. Libraries often have long runs of the documents in microform and do not enter the market for original printed copies, leaving the field open to collectors. The books themselves lack the charm of fine printing, superior paper, and good bindings, so their drab appearance does not attract the eye. Copies are usually quite worn. For many years they could be bought at very low prices, but as with all antiques there is a fixed supply and a growing market, and some government reports have risen tenfold in as many years.

In addition to the reports of expeditions, issued as Congressional documents, other important books were issued by various federal agencies. Two desirable items are *The Coronado Expedition*, edited by George Parker Winship as the fourteenth annual report of the Bureau of American Ethnology, and *Official Correspondence of James S. Calhoun While Indian Agent at Santa Fe*, edited by Annie H. Abel. Both were issued in Washington. Get the 1896 edition of Winship and the 1915 edition of Abel.

129

There are some rarities for which a collector can only yearn. One is the *Kearny Code,* a set of laws printed in Santa Fe when General Kearny established the military government of occupation in 1846. I know of no copy in private hands; it should be worth at least $15,000 in the original. Although this booklist omits single sheet items in general, two must be included. One is the *Aviso* or notice of intent to open a printshop in Santa Fe in 1834 by the first printer in New Mexico. No known copy exists, but we know that one was printed. The other is its companion *Lista de Ciudadanos* (Santa Fe, 1834), a list of citizens who could serve as a jury panel in any suit involving a printer. About 49 copies of this item survive; several are in the State Archives, some in private hands. Forty-nine seems a large number, but remember that at least 48 copies of the Gutenberg Bible exist.

Any good collection on New Mexico will include a few sets, such as Ralph E. Twitchell's *Leading Facts of New Mexico History* (Cedar Rapids, 1911-17, 5 vols.), also his *Spanish Archives of New Mexico* (Cedar Rapids, 1914, 2 vols.). The *Coronado Historical Series* is another desirable set (Albuquerque, 1940-66, 11 vols. with another still planned).

Another important set is the series of 13 titles issued by the Quivira Society, a book club of

130

scholars, during the years 1929-58. Rarest of these is Henry R. Wagner's bibliography, *The Spanish Southwest* (1937, 2 vols.). Only half of the Quivira series deals with New Mexico; the others deal with adjacent lands, but the true collector wants the full set. A bookman's axiom says that any set is worth 20% more than the total cost of its separate parts, with the increase added because of the hunt. Odd volumes in the Coronado and Quivira sets turn up now and then.

Among books by or about Mountain Men, most experts would recommend Howard L. Conard's *"Uncle Dick" Wootton* (Chicago, 1890) and Jacob Fowler's *Journal* (N. Y., 1898). LeRoy Hafen's 10 vol. set on *Mountain Men and Fur Trade of the Far West* (Glendale, 1965-72) is out of print.

Among range and cattle books, possibly only two or three collectors in New Mexico own a copy of the first cowboy song book ever printed in the nation: Nathan H. "Jack" Thorp's *Songs of the Cowboys* (Estancia, N. M., 1908). Another basic ranch item is William French's *Some Recollections of a Western Ranchman* (N. Y., 1928) and the less scarce recent *Further Recollections* (N. Y., 1965). Here might also be included Richard B. Townshend's *The Tenderfoot in New Mexico* (London, 1923); Charles Siringo's *A Texas Cow-Boy* (Chicago, 1885); Pat Garrett's *Authentic*

131

Life of Billy The Kid (Santa Fe, 1882); and the three volumes of memoirs by Miguel A. Otero (1935-40). The scarcest nature book is Florence M. Bailey's *Birds of New Mexico* (Santa Fe, 1928).

Many or all of the general histories of New Mexico belong in a fine collection, especially those by Ralph E. Twitchell (several titles); H. H. Bancroft (1889); Charles F. Coan (1925, 3 vols.); Benjamin M. Read (1912); Frank D. Reeve (1961, 3 vols.); L. Bradford Prince (1893); Elias Brevoort (1874); William G. Ritch (1885); Helen Haines (1891); and the histories bearing no author's name but done by the Lewis Pub. Co. (Chicago, 1895) and the Pacific States Pub. Co. (1907). There is no need to list full titles; all are "History of New Mexico" in some variation.

Other titles that many bibliographers feel should be in a fine collection are Daniel Tyler's *Concise History of the Mormon Battalion* (Salt Lake City, 1881); Philip St. George Cooke's *Conquest of New Mexico and California* (N. Y., 1878); Susan Magoffin's *Down the Santa Fe Trail* (New Haven, 1926); Henry Inman's *Old Santa Fe Trail* (N. Y., 1897); James F. Meline's *Two Thousand Miles on Horseback* (N. Y., 1867); and W. W. H. Davis's *Spanish Conquest of New Mexico* (Doylestown, Pa., 1869). Also favored are Susan Wallace's *Land of the Pueblos* (Troy,

N. Y., 1889); William G. Ritch's *New Mexico Blue Book* (Santa Fe, 1882); and A. F. A. Bandelier's *Historical Documents Relating to New Mexico* (Wash., 1923, 3 vols., edited by Charles Hackett).

More would include George Griggs, *History of Mesilla Valley* (Las Cruces, 1930); Jean B. Salpointe, *Soldiers of the Cross* (Banning, Cal., 1898); and William B. Napton, *Over the Santa Fe Trail* (Kansas City, 1905).

In spite of New Mexico's bilingual culture, few private collectors seek books printed in Spanish. This is a rich field in itself, and Henry R. Wagner's *The Spanish Southwest*, mentioned among the Quivira Society books, is the best guide. Prices are high, often $3,000 and up, but these early works do turn up at the great auctions. Few of these important works are found anywhere in New Mexico today. Collectors and donors are our best hope.

Some nineteenth century works in Spanish are occasionally within reach. These could include Pedro Bautista Pino's *Exposición sucinta* (Cadiz, 1812), or Antonio Barreiro's *Ojeada sobre Nuevo-Méjico* (Puebla, 1832), and José Escudero's *Noticias. . .de Nuevo Méjico* (Mexico City, 1849). Translations of all three are in *Three New Mexico Chronicles* by H. Bailey Carroll and J. Villasana Haggard (Quivira Society, 1942). And count yourself truly favored if you own even one of the booklets by Padre Antonio José Martínez printed in Santa Fe or Taos, especially his *Cuaderno de ortografía* (Santa Fe, 1834), a little speller, the first book printed in New Mexico. Also scarce, and in English, is Nicholas de Freytas' *The Expedition of. . .Penalosa. . . From Santa Fe* (N. Y., 1882).

All books listed above have risen in price chiefly for what they contain. They have a basic, internal value not subject to the ups and downs of fads or speculation. For example, in the past ten years a fever of speculation has pushed the price of H. M. T. Powell's *The Santa Fe Trail to California* (San Francisco, 1931) from about $250 to $1,500 a copy. It is a beautiful and significant book, but there is no internal reason why it should bring a price higher than that of the finest copy of a first edition of Josiah Gregg's *Commerce of the Prairies*.

This list has been skimpy on books about Indians, arts, outlaws and fiction. Those are fields of special interest. In such fields you can be guided by Lawrence Clark Powell's *Southwestern Century* or his *Heart of the Southwest*, or Saul Cohen's list of his ten favorite novels about New Mexico, which appeared in *New Mexico Magazine*, March 1974.

Even today a serious collector can assemble ninety per cent of the first editions listed above.

 134

No single antiquarian shop has even that portion in shelf stock; it would take perhaps five years and visits to many shops to get them. The final ten per cent could take half a lifetime.

But you need not wait years or spend small fortunes to enjoy most of these books in reprint forms. Many of them, especially the most interesting, are available in facsimile reprints or paperback editions. Such a set of books might not be a collector's collection, but it could be a historian's collection. Approximately 100 books have been listed here, and they would fit on about 18 linear feet of shelves. Every New Mexico library, public or educational, should have such an alcove.

Good hunting!

DESERT THRILLERS AND WHODUNITS

C. L. Sonnichsen

MYSTERY AND suspense have always been a major ingredient of Western fiction—hard cover, soft cover, and in between. For example, hundreds of "quest" stories, following James Fenimore Cooper's "pursuit formula," have kept readers on the edge of their chairs in the past and are still being written in quantities. George C. Gilman (pseudonym of Englishman Terry Harknett) is still adding volumes to the "Edge" series, in which Civil War veteran Joshua Hedges began his violent career by pursuing the murderers of his crippled brother and sending them screaming, one by one, to their deaths. Number 34 of the collection was in circulation in early 1980.

Sheriffs and policemen often created suspense in the early novels, and cowboy detectives, occasionally in pairs, appeared with some frequency. Charles Ballew (pen name Charles H. Snow) assigned his sleuthing to a pair of oddballs named Slats Kennedy and Rimfire Boggs (*The Bandit of the Paloduro*, 1934). Hashknife

Hartley was the brainchild of W. C. Tuttle (*Tumbling River Range*, 1935). Tuttle also wrote the "Henry" series, featuring Sheriff Henry Harrison Conroy (*Wildhorse Valley*, 1938). The Texas Rangers were represented in the Jack Slade series issued under the name of Bradford Scott.

In more recent years we have Brian Garfield's *The Threepersons Hunt* (1974), in which Arizona State Trooper Sam Watchman, a Navajo, corrals a murderer on the unfriendly White Mountain Apache Reservation. Bill Burchardt's *Buck* (1978) follows the sheriff as he tames an Oklahoma oil town, and the new sexual freedom has brought us the Longarm series, mass produced (a book a month) by several writers using the house name Tabor Evans. *Longarm and the Sheepherders* (1980) is number 21 in the lineup. Deputy Marshal Custis Long pursues criminals and women all over the pioneer West with equal success in the bushes and in the bedroom. A hundred examples of embattled lawmen looking for the real murderer could easily be cited.

Something new, however, is being added. Even a casual check of *Publishers Weekly*, the book review periodicals, or even the revolving racks in the corner drugstore will reveal the amazing number of suspense novels, unconnected with the Wild West tradition, now being written in the Southwest. Arizona, New Mexico and Texas provide plenty of examples in half a dozen categories.

Let's start with town-oriented murder mysteries. They go back a long way, at least as far as Frances Crane's *The Turquoise Shop* (1941) set in Santa Fe, or Dorothy Hughes' Santa Fe murder mystery *Ride the Pink Horse* (1946, reissued by Bantam, 1979). Frederick Brown's *The Far Cry,* with a Taos setting, was written in 1951, and in 1954 Norman Hales treated the people of Santa Fe to *The Spider in the Cup,* a *roman à clef* about a once-famous local murder. Everybody knew who was who and who did what. Austin, Texas, enjoyed a similar experience when Olivia Dwight published *Close His Eyes* (1960), about a drunken English poet who was murdered on the university campus. Important people on the faculty, with all their eccentricities spotlighted, were part of the cast. The author's professor husband lost his job— not, the administrators said, because of his wife's book but because he had violated the rules by advertising his house for sale on the faculty bulletin board.

Later examples would include *Don't Open the Door* (1968) by Ursula Curtiss, set in Albuquerque; Phyllis A. Whitney, *The Turquoise Mask* (1974) with a Santa Fe locale; Elizabeth Peters' *The Summer of the Dragon* (1979)

138

exploiting the picturesque Sedona, Arizona, area; and *Vampire Tapestry* by Susie Charnis (1980), with the Santa Fe opera in the background.

Mystery writers include a number of practitioners in the area of occult and supernatural. In 1977 James Norman published *The Obsidian Mirror,* in which a Mexican protagonist moves between the sixteenth and twentieth centuries. The following year Marlys Millhiser struck a similar chord with *The Mirror,* in which central character Shay, on her wedding night, is taken back a century to inhabit her grandmother's body in a Western mining camp. Grandma, meanwhile, has to settle for Shay's body—an ordeal for her since she is a straightlaced Victorian and Shay is three months pregnant. This sort of time travel reappears in Stephanie Blake's *Secret Sins* (1978) in which Mara Tate, head of an Arizona copper empire, relives the lives of her mother and grandmother. Her experiences include an affair with Wyatt Earp.

A somewhat larger category includes a number of fine novels dealing with ordeals in which survival is the main issue and the suspense is terrific. James Hall Roberts' *The Burning Sky* (1966) is an excellent example. A group of white men and women are trapped in a hidden village of extremely primitive Indians near Tucson and survive almost by a miracle.

Ten years later (1976) Lucinda Baker wrote *The Place of Devils*, featuring a tenderfoot girl on the Navajo reservation who marries an older man and almost becomes the victim of his Navajo first wife. In 1976 also, the Gordons (man and wife team) authored *Ordeal*, in which a girl survives a plane crash in Navajoland with a fortune in jewels and a slim chance of survival.

The heartbeats come faster with Martin Cruz Smith's terrific thriller *Nightwing* (1977) about an invasion of vampire bats from Mexico, threatening an epidemic of bubonic plague in Arizona. Just as gripping is *Fear in a Handful of Dust*, by John Ives (1978). A madman escapes from confinement and rounds up five psychiatrists, men and women, who had put him behind bars. He leaves them without food, water or clothing in the Arizona desert near the Mexican border and waits for them to die. They disappoint him. A superior example of the ordeal type is Richard Martin Stern's *Snowbound Six* (1978), which recounts the sufferings and inner growth of travelers marooned by a snowstorm in the mountains near Santa Fe. More good novels appeared in 1979. Walter Kendrick contributed *Fire in the Sky*, which tells what happens when a comet destroys Phoenix, and James L. Stowe wrote "a riveting novel of violence and psycho-sexual suspense," *Winter Stalk*. Their car out of commission, two young people in the New Mexico wilderness need help for their sick, adopted child and are taken in by Michael, an eccentric recluse. Michael gets out of hand and the two have a narrow, blood-spattered escape.

1980 produced more nerve-shattering ordeals. Eddie Macon, in *Eddie Macon's Run,* is jailed on a false charge, escapes, and runs 108 miles to the Mexican border. *Publishers Weekly* calls James McLendon "an uncommonly suspenseful writer" who can "mesmerize" the reader. In similarly glowing terms it calls Marilyn Harris' *The Portent* "A properly nightmarish doomsday book; a dandy of its kind." Harris brings several young people from Boston to seek an idyllic life in a remote Rocky Mountain village. Nature wants them out and nearly does them in.

A much wider vein opens in the area involving spies, intrigues, undercover agents and international machinations. My list includes twenty such novels just since 1976. Corruption in Washington reaches a clammy hand into the West Texas desert in George La Fountaine's *Flashpoint* (1976), and threatens two honest, hard-drinking, woman chasing border patrolmen when they come upon a well-heeled skeleton in a carefully concealed jeep, somehow connected with the Kennedy assassination. In

Philip Chase's *Merchants of Death* (1976), the presence of a Multipurpose Unmanned Tactical Airborne Weapons System in a hideout near Tucson brings on international activity and concern.

In Hartshorne's *The Mexican Assassin* (1978), Lee Barber of the CIA, a James Bond type, investigates a political assassination in Mexico and just misses being wiped out himself. Hartshorne (a pseudonym) writes a good thriller, but his real object is to expose the duplicity and corruption of the U. S. secret services. Campbell Black, in *Asterisk Destiny* (1978), centers on a mysterious object (Asterisk) under guard in the desert near Phoenix. Thorne, a minor White House official, is sent to investigate. The solution is unbelievable, but the pace is fast. In Lawrence Dunning's *Keller's Bomb* (1978), David Keller and his girl friend are abducted from a Texas campus and held in Santa Fe by a band of Argentine terrorists who force him to produce a nuclear weapon with which they plan to blackmail the U. S. government.

David Alexander in *The Chocolate Spy* (1978) focuses on an organic computer (Chocolate), half way between a man and a machine, who will rule the world if not stopped. FBI Agent Frank Merriman and the Soviets share in the action. *Phoenix No More* (1978), by Edwin Gage, is a powerful anti-nukes document disguised as a good suspense novel. Powerful men in Arizona want an atomic power plant near Phoenix. Concerned citizens risk their lives to defeat them.

In Suzanne Morris' *Keeping Secrets* (1979), Camille Devera is secretary to a German-born banker in San Antonio during World War I. He is financing a venture in Mexico by Texan Emory Cabot. Camille spies on her employer and uncovers much unexpected information. *The Ogden Enigma* (1980), by Gene Snyder, begins and ends at a small military base in Utah. Academician and writer Ted Lawrence gets possession of a small object resembling a fountain pen which can cause blackouts over half a city. Agents and double agents provide a really suspenseful tale. Hair-raising events follow the crash of a newly designed airplane in Jack Bickham's *The Excalibur Disaster* (1980).

In Mark Elder's *The Prometheus Operation* (1980), Abwehr agent Stefan Roebling is sent from Europe to locate the U. S. facility for developing the atomic bomb. American agent Greg Allison pursues him. The denouement comes at Los Alamos. Action starts in the Austin, Texas, airport in Robert Ray's *Cage of Mirrors* (1980) where a photographer is murdered. His friend Taggard, sponsored by a Texas billionaire and the U. S. government (who have their own motives), pursues the killers to

143

New York and Europe, involving himself with the international diamond cartel and a gang of super thieves. In *The Sonora Mutation* (1980), by Albert J. Elias, a New York detective and a government botanist try to trace a shipment of contaminated heroin, cause of death for hundreds of people in the East, to its source in Mexico.

The indefatigable Edward Abbey, in *Good News* (1980), having warned us Southwesterners that our water is going to run out, now visualizes what happens when it does. The Arizona economic system has collapsed. Easterners in droves go back where they came from. A dictator has taken over Phoenix, hanging and torturing his enemies. A retired professor and a Harvard-educated Hopi take him on. *Limbo* by Joel Hammil (1980) is a California item, but it deserves mention. A government-subsidized "mind-control" experiment in Southern California picks "patients" by computer and subjects them to brain surgery. They are supposed to emerge as geniuses but all, at the time of the story, have become vegetables. Connie Keegan, a tough New York prostitute, brings her doctor with her, but she is on the operating table before he and his connections can get any action.

A particularly interesting (and my last) category involves outright detective stories, complete with sleuth. The private eye may be amateur or professional, but he observes, reasons and pursues in the manner of Sherlock Holmes. And, believe it or not, Sherlock himself appears—twice—on the Southwestern scene.

An early example of the type, published in 1940, was the first of Marjorie Boniface's two whodunits called *Murder as an Ornament*. Hiram Odom, authentic West Texas sheriff, is called in to find out who killed an expendable woman named Charmian on Christmas Eve. Thirty years later one of the best of the recent writers made his debut. That was Tony Hillerman in *The Blessingway* (1970), where Joe Leaphorn, the Navajo policeman and detective, is introduced. In this and subsequent novels Tony bases his story on Navajo customs and lore. His latest is *People of Darkness* (1980). This time the detective is Sergeant Jim Chee of the Navajo Tribal Police.

In *Murder in the Walls* (1971), by Richard Martin Stern, Johnny Ortiz, part Apache and part Spanish-American, solves a murder mystery in Santa Fe which involves a parlor house dating back to 1620. Stern is socially conscious as well as a fine writer. He has abandoned detective stories for more ambitious projects, but he was one of the best in the business. In Shepard Rifkin's *The Snow Rattlers* (1976), McQuaid, a tough New York detective, is called in to find a murderer who has stolen some priceless Indian art objects. The trail leads to New Mexico and the end comes at the Zuni Shalako ceremony. Rifkin knows more about New York than he does about New Mexico, but he tells a good story.

Sughrue, a melancholy alcoholic private investigator in James Crumley's *The Last Good Kiss* (1978), teams up with permanently drunk writer Abraham Traherne to find Betty Sue, missing for ten years. The search takes them to barrooms and bedrooms all over the West. In John Reese's *Weapon Heavy* (1973), Jefferson Hewitt, frontier detective, comes to Dunsmuir, Kansas, to look for two suspected killers. He encounters a variety of oddballs, including Elsie, who has "brains enough to run the Bank of England" and "no more conscience than a tarantula." Reese has used Hewitt in several books, the latest being *Two Thieves and a Puma* (1980).

Glendon Swarthout's 13th book, *Skeletons* (1980), is his first detective story and recounts the adventures of B. James Butters, an "adorable" writer of children's books. He visits New Mexico, at the request of his ex-wife, to dig up some facts about her background and turns up several nasty skeletons. George Simenon's great French detective Maigret investigates the death of a promiscuous teenager near Tucson in *Maigret at the Coroners* (1980). In *Enter the*

Lion (1980) by Michael P. Hodel and Sean M. Wright, Mycroft Holmes and his younger brother Sherlock solve a case "found" in a Los Angeles antique shop. According to *Publishers Weekly*, Edmund Aubrey has done "a superb job" in *Sherlock Holmes in Dallas* (1980), where Holmes works on the Kennedy assassination. Finally, in Don Pendleton's *Arizona Ambush* (The Executioner, No. 31, 1980), Mack Bolan, trained as a killer in South Vietnam, takes on the Mafia in Arizona. In thirty previous books he has taken on "the forces of evil" almost everywhere else. This book is a good argument for the view that the western is being challenged by the suspense novel.

C. L. Sonnichsen, former Professor and Dean at Texas Western College (now University of Texas at El Paso), author of many books on Southwestern history, is now living in Tucson, where he is Senior Editor of "The Journal of Arizona History."

THE FUTURE OF THE BOOK
IN NEW MEXICO

Dwight A. Myers

IN THE LAST 100 years of New Mexico's near-450-year "book history," we have seen a growing symbiotic relationship between the book and the state. The natural gifts the land offers the creative mind have attracted more superb talent than per capita statistics would allow could happen. The intellectual and physical climate that a Taos, a Cerrillos or even a Quemado offers is most certainly our greatest resource.

As the intellectual climate goes, so go the fortunes of those involved in the book, whether librarian, bookseller, printer, publisher or collector. We do have giant gaps as far as bookstores are concerned, with 14 of our 32 counties having no bookstores at all. Some one of our enterprising booksellers will develop a mail order system, using the local newspaper to reach these people. It is possible that our authors might travel in small groups, sponsored by the local publisher and a local bookstore. On arriving in a storeless town, each would give a short presentation, followed by an autographing session. I could envision the local school or the community fathers helping this touring group by providing a place for the event and even some funds to defray expenses.

Where there is no bookstore but there is a public library, that library might become involved. But for towns where there are neither library nor bookstores, it would have to involve the school or business community. Other innovations I can foresee are traveling bookstores just as we have library bookmobiles, more book rental sections in established bookstores (perhaps even renting by mail), far fewer hardbacks and far more paperbacks in the stores, more national chain booksellers. The stores that stress personal service and true involvement with their customers are the ones that will survive.

Our libraries will continue to have an economic struggle until we establish a system of local levy or tax that will become a dependable monetary base from year to year. Our public libraries have found it increasingly difficult to keep up with the new literature and general book needs of their communities. Many of the smaller ones are able to buy only 100 to 500 new books a year, or fewer than a third of 1% of the new books available. I do trust that part of the future of books in New Mexico will be

149

a legislated, dependable tax-based funding program for public libraries.

Our libraries, especially the college and university libraries, have one foot through the electronic-age door. This allows for simplified processing to get books on the shelf faster. It also will allow, in the not too distant future, easy access to information not in that library in print form. The computer is revolutionizing the library world; but New Mexico, with its small economic base, will have to wait a long while for data retrieval systems already available to many public libraries. The book as we know it now will most certainly survive. No electronic system can replace pleasure reading, simply the friendly companionship the book affords. The future library in New Mexico will be part electronic, part book; but no library will become 100% electronic—not in New Mexico!

The publishing future of New Mexico is very healthy. There are no rich publishers here nor will there ever be. But small publishers will continue to grow at a leisurely pace. Large national firms find it increasingly difficult to produce a book that has a potential sale of under 5,000 copies. The small publisher is filling the void. I don't expect to see any bookstores get into publishing as was so popular in the 1930s, but it wouldn't surprise me if a few did give it a try.

If you would agree to define a publisher as

150

one who produces at least two books a year, you might be surprised to find that we have almost 50 such enterprises in our state at this writing. In the period 1975-80 we had more new publishers than new bookstores. With one or two exceptions, they do not print the books they sell; they choose titles, edit and design the book and market it. Most of the books are printed and bound outside the state. New Mexico suffers from the lack of full book printing and binding facilities. I would hope that soon one of our printer-manufacturers would find it economically feasible to obtain essential machinery for the binding process.

Book reviewing is in a state of disorder in New Mexico and is unlikely to improve in the near future. Most book reviewers in New Mexico are unpaid volunteers. A few in-state magazines review books and the *New Mexico Magazine* has been doing so for many years. But we know of no radio or television book reviewing at present, though we hope this will be in their future plans. We would hope that some enterprising group of people will begin a free book-reviewing service for the many small newspapers in the state, and that newspapers will be open to such a proposal. It is surprising that the largest book organization in the state, the New Mexico Library Association, doesn't even review books in their newsletter.

In the future of the book in New Mexico there are still many gaps. We lack funds for a truly healthy public library or even academic library system. The number of bookstores is limited. We have a barely adequate information flow as far as new book reviews and information are concerned. But we have abundant writing talent, the prime resource. We have many healthy small publishers. And all the weaknesses can be overcome should our people so demand. It is a bright future in general. But it will not be met without a struggle and a great deal of love, sweat and tears.

Dwight A. Myers is the founder and Executive Director of the New Mexico Book League. After a short association with the University of New Mexico Bookstore, he joined Prentice-Hall Publishing Company, becoming Assistant Vice-President of their General Book Marketing Division. Dwight and his wife Carol, who is the Sales Manager of the University of New Mexico Press, live in Albuquerque.

PART TWO

The Question:

What three books have had the greatest impact on your life, and why?

The Answers:

The responses of seventy-six prominent New Mexicans are on the following pages, appearing in alphabetical order by name of respondent.

Editors' Note:

The contributors to this section of our book are to be commended for their courage. The question is a very personal one, and the answers revealing. For their kind cooperation and sincere contributions, we thank them.

GEORGE AGOGINO

Educator, anthropologist, at Eastern New Mexico University, Portales.

Loren Eisley's *The Immense Journey* is the story of human evolution, brilliantly written with the skill of a scientist and the soul of a philosopher. The story of man's achievements and the development for the last several million years made me realize that many great adventures and discoveries have been made by individuals who have never received credit for their achievements.

The Phenomenon of Man by Father Teilhard de Chardin made compatible to me Christianity and the theory of human evolution. I retained my Christian beliefs while accumulating much scientific knowledge in the field of human evolution.

Finally I would name John Reed's *Insurgent Mexico*. This book concentrates on the Mexican revolution, 1910-14, where Reed served as a war correspondent. Its unique approach deals with the foot soldiers rather than the generals. It made me see more clearly the role of the "little man" in uncontrollable world events.

RUDOLFO A. ANAYA

Author and professor at the University of New Mexico, his works include *Bless Me Ultima*, *Heart of Aztlán*, *Tortuga* and *Cuentos: Tales From the Hispanic Southwest*.

It is difficult for me to pick the three books which have made the greatest impact on my life. What I suggest to young people is that they read as much as possible. The "touchstone theory" took me to the great literature of the world, and to serious, contemporary literature. I was also influenced by the oral literary tradition when I was growing up, and that rich source should not be discounted. Young people—indeed, all of us —should listen more to the stories of those with age and wisdom on their side.

PHELPS ANDERSON

Businessman, rancher, living near Roswell.

The answer to your question is most difficult; however, I would offer the following three works as having great impact on my life.

Catch 22 by Joseph Heller is a novel describing a comic fact of life. I never cease to be amazed at how often I encounter this one fact of life—catch 22—during my family, business and political endeavors.

Foundation, a trilogy by Isaac Asimov, is

160

solid gold science fiction and a fascinating, at least for me, futuristic view of mankind.

Perhaps my third choice would be *Jonathan Livingston Seagull* by Richard Bach. This beautiful story captured my imagination, as I have often dreamed of flying like the birds. Since my early years I have enjoyed ornithology and the outdoors. This story is what I hope it would have been like had I really been a bird of feathers.

RUTH ARMSTRONG

Author of *Enchanted Land: New Mexico* (1973) and *New Mexico* (2nd edition, 1975), as well as frequent contributions to many periodicals.

This was fun. I guess I'd have to say these have had the greatest influence on my life, though tomorrow I may well think of a half-dozen more.

The *Rubaiyat of Omar Khayyam* translated by Edward Fitzgerald (Garden City Pub. Co.), has been special to me since my early 20s. It has been a comfort, solace and a lyrical beauty that fills me with pleasure.

The *Literature of England* by Woods, Watt and Anderson (Scott, Foresman & Co.), is a textbook that I had in my first year of college, but it is my favorite textbook of all time. I still refer to it frequently. It not only has excerpts

161

from many of my favorite authors, but good introductions to literary periods from the Romantic Movement to the first World War.

I consider *Great River* by Paul Horgan (Rinehart & Co.) to be the best and most comprehensive history of New Mexico, and a bible to me in my writing. It is a pleasure to read, too.

LURA BENNETT

Lifetime teacher and Past President of the New Mexico Retired Teachers Association. Now living in Raton.

Here are three unforgettable books experienced in my lifetime.

Ben Hur by Lew Wallace was read in mid-adolescence and brought all Biblical literature out of a religious haze and made that era credible as being inhabited by working, suffering, rejoicing, noble and base human beings.

Tale of Two Cities by Charles Dickens explored a world of unbelievable social injustice in which force was the only "right" recognized in any political structure.

Death Comes For the Archbishop by Willa Cather brought to me a great appreciation of the timeless quality of New Mexico and the vastly different contributions made by its three human cultures.

JEFF BINGAMAN

Attorney General, the State of New Mexico.

The three books that come to mind which have been significant to me are: *The Wind in the Willows* by Kenneth Graham, always a favorite of mine, which I find a welcome respite from the real world. *Morning and Noon* is a biographical description of Dean Acheson's early life, including his early years in Washington. I find the highminded description of Washington life in those days to be inspiring. *The Effective Executive* is a book I have recently read which seems to contain very sound advice for people in my present position. I believe Peter Drucker has correctly identified the five most significant habits which any executive must form in order to succeed.

HELEN BLUMENSCHEIN

Artist, living in Taos.

Old Jules, published in the 1930s, had a lifelong influence on my love for vegetable gardening. Then *Leonardo Da Vinci's Diary*, translated in the 1930s, influenced me in my philosophy towards art: in its variation, not any one line. Finally, Dr. Paul Sears' *While There Is Life* influenced my thinking towards nature.

163

JEANNE BONNETTE

Poet. Published *Colored Sails* (1930), *Seven Stars* (1939) and *Leaf Change* (1979), among others. Her poetry has appeared in many periodicals.

In naming the following three, please know that I am leaving out many others.

In my twenties I was much impressed with Edna St. Vincent Millay's *Fatal Interview* (Harper Brothers, 1931). The language is more than excellent, and the emotions are deep.

Kristin Lavransdatter by Sigrid Undset, the trilogy of 13th century Norway (Knopf, 1927), was probably most memorable to me in my thirties. From it I learned great history.

My third choice is *Raintree County* by Ross Lockridge, Jr., (Houghton Mifflin). The flow of the writing, the power of its irony, the innocence of love make this book my favorite work of fiction. I realize that Undset's book was also fiction, but it contained much historical fact and information, so that I think of it as a learning book and *Raintree County* as pure fiction.

WILLIAM J. BUCHANAN

Author of *A Shining Season*, later made into a television movie. Also published in *True*, *The Reader's Digest*, *Mankind*, *American Heritage* and many other periodicals.

 164

The Big Sky by A. B. Guthrie, Jr., is a remarkable feat of imagination. It chronicled the "West that was" for me as no other book before or since. The fact that it was written by an easterner (whom I knew when I was a lad growing up in Kentucky) taught me a lasting lesson about the value of detailed research to a working author.

Jonathan Livingston Seagull by Richard Bach was scornfully rejected by scores of editors but, once published, became a phenomenal best seller which prompted *The Reader's Digest,* among others, to publicly apologize for failing to recognize its merits earlier. By no means one of my favorites, the book nonetheless reaffirmed my faith to persist against negative editorial judgments, a practice that has paid off handsomely time and time again.

My final choice must be *A Shining Season* by William Buchanan. It paid my debts.

RICHARD BUHLER

Bookseller. Owner of Brotherhood of Life Metaphysical Bookstore, Albuquerque's oldest such book outlet.

After giving your question considerable thought, I would first name *A Study of History* by Arnold J. Toynbee, 2 volume set. These books not only outline history, but show the mechanics and the philosophical flux and flow of man's organized stint on earth.

Second would be *Coronado's Children* by J. Frank Dobie. Its tales of lost treasure and gold in the Southwest brought out the adventurous spirit in me.

My list ends with *The Bhagavad Gita* (Gita Press edition). This Hindu Bible is an epic dialogue between Krishna and Arjuna, which brought to me direct understanding of day-to-day living and how that is translated into a cosmic form lifetime after lifetime.

ALICE BULLOCK

Author of many books about the Southwest, including *Living Legends, The Squaw Tree, Northern New Mexico Villages*. Photographer and book reviewer, now living in Santa Fe.

Every book read leaves an impact of some kind, good or bad. My favorites, however, date back to my youth.

Anne of Green Gables was not only a favorite because of the character, but because here for the first time I found that characters did not necessarily cease to exist when one came to "The End." They could be found in sequels. This fact gave more life to reading and authenticity to the people I liked in books.

Complete Arithmetic by Wentworth and

Smith was a book I hated with a vengeance from the fifth through the eighth grade. After I had my eighth grade diploma, I kept the book just to thumb my nose at. When I began to teach in rural schools, it held my hand through all kinds of crises. I couldn't get along without it!

Reflections of A Lonely Man, no author given, (McClurg, 1903). I picked this up in a bushel basket of books at Acres of Books in Long Beach, California. It has the homespun philosophy that sounds new each time it is read. It is heavily underlined and annotated by my contentions as a young woman and still comforts me as an old lady. Not bad for just ten cents!

JETTA CARLETON

Author of the novel, *The Moonflower Vine,* and editor for The Lightning Tree, Santa Fe.

In a backwoods culture, where the poetry available to us was, for the most part, rhymed homily, a teacher loaned me a copy of *New Voices: An Introduction to Contemporary Poetry,* by Marguerite Wilkinson (Macmillan, 1931; 1st edition 1919). Much of it quaint by today's standards, but I had never seen anything like it. It was a revelation (and about time, too!)

In *Modern American Poets,* selected by

Conrad Aiken (Modern Library, 1927), I discovered Aiken's own lyrics, which illumined my youth, and Wallace Stevens, who continues to baffle and enchant me more than any other poet.

Reluctantly I skip Proust, Thoreau and the virtuosity of *Nightwood* by Djuna Barnes (New Directions, 1946; Harcourt, 1936) in favor of Joyce's *Portrait of the Artist as a Young Man*. I just love it, that's why.

MARSIE CATE

Santa Fe art gallery and bookstore owner, book reviewer and avid craftsperson.

The first book was Ole Edvart Rolvaag's *Giants in the Earth*. I received it as a prize for having read the most books in summer camp. It was my first prize for doing something I loved and also introduced me to the great expanse of the midwest. The second book was Jean Vercors' *You Shall Know Them*. This is about the killing of an offspring that was half human, half anthropoid. Was it murder or a simple killing of an animal? If not murder, then animals could be produced as slaves with human attributes.

The third was Jan Morris' *Conundrum*. Her story of her sex change was told so beautifully and in such depth that I think everyone

168

should read it and develop a sense of what the various sex roles are.

FRAY ANGELICO CHAVEZ

Author, historian, poet, retired Catholic priest, now living in Santa Fe. He was book reviewer for many years for the *New Mexico Magazine*. Among his many books are: *My Penitente Land*, *Reflections on Spanish New Mexico*, *Origins of New Mexico Families*, *La Conquistadora*, *New Mexico Triptych*, *The Single Rose*.

No one particular book made any great impression on my child and boyhood years, just a set of encyclopedias during the grammar school years. It was an old set of some ten thick volumes which my father owned. It was not the Britannica, but did carry the name "American" or "Columbia"—can't recall which. Last time I saw the set was at age fourteen, when I left home for school in Ohio. But I can assure you that I read the whole set, back and forth, during those eight grammar school years, especially in winter, since we kids in those days had no radio, no library, no movies, no school gyms and no extracurricular school activities. And the winters in Mora, New Mexico, were cold as hell!

169

PEGGY POND CHURCH

Author of many works, including *The House at Otowi Bridge* and *The Ripened Fields: Fifteen Sonnets of a Marriage*. Her father, Ashley Pond, was the founder of the Los Alamos Ranch School in 1917. She resides in Santa Fe.

Without hesitation I will name first *A Child's Garden of Verses* by Robert Louis Stevenson, in the edition illustrated by Jessie Wilcox Smith and published (I think) by Scribner's about 1910. I think it most likely that I caught my incurable addiction to the sound and rhythm of poetry from this book.

Next in order, probably, though much later, is *The Golden Bough* by J. G. Frazer, the one volume edition (Macmillan, 1922). This was given me by an elderly cousin, a bibliophile, around 1925. It gave me a new way of looking at the world, opening my imagination and understanding to the universality of seasonal myths and rituals, and helped me appreciate more wisely the ceremonies of our Pueblo Indians, as well as much English literature—and even my own dreams!

My third choice is the most difficult. I will cheat a little and mention the *Collected Works of William Blake* in the Random House edition and all the bilingual editions of Pablo Neruda's poetry, *Las alturas de Macchu Picchu*, translated by Nathaniel Tarn.

 170

But for real *impact,* coming with the force of revelation and never ceasing to reverberate in my life, I think I must choose *The Secret of the Golden Flower* (Harcourt Brace & Co., 1932). This I value almost entirely for the European commentary by C. G. Jung, which opened to me the vast world of the unconscious and the play of opposites in my own nature and in all poetry, "the polarity inherent in all life."

SAUL COHEN

Attorney and counselor-at-law, living in Santa Fe. Author of *Scholarly Publishing and the Law* and many articles of special interest to Southwestern bibliophiles.

Trying to seriously answer the question, one of the books which came to mind was Harvey Fergusson's *The Conquest of Don Pedro.* This is not because of its content, but because it was the first Harvey Fergusson work which I read, and it started me on collecting Fergusson works, which has been a source of great pleasure for me. Another work which had some impact is *The Education of a Poker Player* by Herbert Yardley. Not only is it a delightful book, but it improved my game tremendously. Then there's *Orthotherapy* by Dr. Arthur Michele, a book on the back which I highly recommend to all lower back sufferers.

There are books that one feels one could justify mentioning but without conviction that they are truly among the three that had the greatest impact: Edith Hamilton's works on Greece, or Arthur Conan Doyle's *Through the Magic Door*. Others would include Herbert Muller's *The Uses of the Past*, James Harvey Robinson's *The Mind in the Making*, Rene Dubos' *So Human an Animal*, Homer Smith's *Man and His Gods*, Arthur Koestler's *Darkness at Noon*, J. Frank Dobie's *Life and Literature of the Southwest*, F. S. C. Northrop's *The Meeting of East and West*, Zechariah Chafee's *Free Speech in the United States*, Vincent Sheean's *Personal History*, Clyde Kluckhohn's *Mirror for Man*, David Mellinkoff's *The Language of the Law*, and Lawrence Clark Powell's *Books in My Baggage*.

ROGER B. CORBETT

Former President, New Mexico State University, Las Cruces.

The only book that truly had a great impact on me was a little paperback called *Main Spring* published about fifty years ago. It "sold" me on the free enterprise system. I loaned it once too often. No other book stands out.

 172

FRANK J. CROSBY

Businessman, sportsman, living in Albuquerque. For years he has presented home furnishings and recreational living shows, as well as various sports shows.

The books that made the most impact on me and my life are: *Think and Grow Rich* by Napoleon Hill (Hawthorne Pub. Co., 1966); *Psycho-Cybernetics* by Maxwell Maltz (Prentice-Hall, 1960); and *Magic Power of Your Mind* by Walter Germain (Wilshire Book Co.). As you can see, I almost exclusively enjoy books relating to the subject of metaphysics or autobiographical material of successful persons. I rarely read fiction of any kind.

BABA RAM DASS

Author of *Be More Now*. Leading metaphysician, resident of Santa Fe.

These three books have all deepened my spiritual understandings and my love for God:

The Bhagavad Gita (Penguin edition), Juan Mascaro, editor.

The Tao Te Ching by Lao Tze (Mentor Books).

Hsin Hsin Ming, Richard Clark translator (Coachman Press of Canada).

WILLIAM E. DAVIS

Former president, University of New Mexico,
Albuquerque.

I read the three volumes of *Lee's Lieutenants* by Douglas S. Freeman while learning to be a Marine officer at Quantico, Virginia. They not only sharpened an appreciation for the principles of leadership, but also whetted my appetite for a deeper study of history.

Then I shall never forget *Barefoot Boy With Cheek* by Max Shulman. My fraternity brothers and I read this aloud while I was in college and literally rolled on the floor laughing. It was the beginning of a long-standing interest in campus humor.

Finally I would name *The Art of War* by Sun-Tzu. This has been invaluable in my sixteen years as a university president.

EDWIN J. DELATTRE

President, St. John's College, Santa Fe, New
Mexico.

No three books by themselves have made the greatest impact on my life; but three books which have influenced me greatly are Plato's *Gorgias*, which is a striking account of the place of reasoned discourse in human life; Immanuel Kant's *Fundamental Principles of the Metaphysics of Morals*, which is a lucid explanation of principled conduct; and Gilbert Highet's *The Art of Teaching*, the best book on teaching written in America in the twentieth century.

STEPHEN R. DONALDSON

An Albuquerque resident and author of fantasy novels, including the three volume *The Chronicles of Thomas Covenant.*

Since I now write epic fantasy novels with "adventure-story" surfaces, intricately structured plots and imagery, and what we used to call "high moral seriousness," I guess you could say that these three books have certainly had an impact on my life.

Joseph Conrad's *Heart of Darkness,* aside from being one of the most complex and finely-crafted novellas ever written, demonstrates just how much depth can lie hidden beneath an adventure-story surface.

The Wings of the Dove by Henry James, a long and occasionally diffuse novel, is nevertheless almost a textbook example of the ways in which plot and imagery can be structured to enhance a story.

Lord of the Rings by J. R. R. Tolkien, a classic (perhaps *the* classic) of its type, shows how much emotional force the pure beauty of fantasy can generate.

175

ROSALIE F. DOOLITTLE

Author of the long-time best selling gardening book in New Mexico, *Southwest Gardening*.

Valley of Decision by Marcia Davenport would be my first choice. I cannot give a good reason except that it was written so well and is a fine account of American life. *The Robe* by Lloyd C. Douglas would be my second choice. Finally, *Roses for Every Garden* by R. C. Allen (M. Barrows & Co., 1948) would be my third choice. There are many fine books on roses but after these many years, this one is still up to date in its contents. It inspired me to truly get involved with the fine hobby of gardening and eventually to write *Southwest Gardening*.

DON DRESP

Librarian, Thomas Branigan Memorial Library in Las Cruces. Past President, New Mexico Library Association.

Nicholas and Alexandra by Robert K. Massie (Atheneum, 1967), is the finest biography I have ever read. The human story of a devoted family and the tragedies that befell them left an emotional and historical impact on me.

While in high school I read Edna Ferber's *So Big* (Doubleday, 1923). It left me in tears as I read this human family story set in Texas.

My third choice is *The Eighth Day* by

Thornton Wilder (Harper, 1967). Mr. Wilder checked into a hotel in Douglas, Arizona, and spent one year in his room writing the original manuscript. This book is the most gripping, well written and thoughtful novel I have ever read.

CONCHA ENCINIAS

Librarian at the Moise Memorial Library of Santa Rosa, New Mexico.

The three I have chosen I have read within the past ten years, even though they carry older copyrights: *My Shadow Ran Fast* by Bill Sands (Prentice-Hall, 1965); *Vivien Leigh* by Anne Edwards (Simon and Schuster, 1977); and *Desiree* by Annemarie Selinko (William Morrow, 1953). The main characters in these books are fine examples of people who have accomplished much through determination, despite the ever present insurmountable obstacles. I found them to be an inspiration.

RICHARD W. ETULAIN

Editor, *New Mexico Historical Review.*

The *Bible* has had more impact on my life than any other book. When I was in grade school, my mother read Bible stories to me and to my brothers, and the narrative drive and live-

177

liness of the historical occurrences, especially those in the Old Testament, whetted my interest in the tug of literature and the drama of history. But the influence of the Bible has also been personal; I still find in that book philosophies of life that I strive to fulfill.

Professionally, Henry Nash Smith's *Virgin Land: The American West as Symbol and Myth* (1950) has shaped my thinking. Smith's stimulating book shows that the myths about the West are as important as historical events for an understanding of the region.

I think Wallace Stegner's *Angle of Repose* (1971) is the most significant novel written about the West in the last three or four decades. It ranks with John Steinbeck's *Grapes of Wrath* and the novels of Willa Cather as premier fictional interpretations of the American West.

GEORGE H. EWING

Director, Museum Division, Office of Cultural Affairs of the State of New Mexico.

I had hoped that if I were to hide quietly beneath my desk you'd think me gone and cease your importunate query. How does one select three crucial links from a chain extending back to childhood?

Many years ago I had access to the complete works of Shakespeare. In it I discovered the beauty and excitement of the written word. It created an addiction.

Plato's *Dialogues* opened an entirely new dimension to me—a new perspective on examination of the human condition and an appreciation of the timelessness of Man's concern with self and universe.

And finally, C. W. Ceram's *Gods, Graves, and Scholars* brought my own interests into focus, sent me back to school, led me into anthropology and eventually into the museum world.

G. WARD FENLEY

"Mr. Action Line," the Albuquerque *Journal*.

I would first have to name Sir Walter Scott's *Quentin Durward* (1824), followed by Cervantes' *Don Quixote* (1605-1615), and finally Victor Hugo's *Les Miserables* (1862).

Having read only parts of it, I never considered *Quentin Durward* my bosom companion. However, my parents were reading it in 1901 when I was born, and they were so impressed that they gave me my name from Durward—the "Ward" part of it.

Don Quixote thrilled me with the practicality of Sancho and the idealism of Don Quixote.

Les Miserables was, likewise, a thriller with confrontations between Javert and Jean Valjean.

179

GENE FRUMKIN

Author of many books including *The Hawk and the Lizard* (Swallow), *The Orange Tree* (Cyfoeth) and *Locust City* (San Marcos); poetry published in *Paris Review*, *New Mexico Magazine*, *Evergreen* and *Saturday Review*. Professor, University of New Mexico.

My first choice would be *The Brothers Karamazov* by Fyodor Dostoyevsky as translated by David Magarshack (Penguin Books). This novel, which I read in my early 20s, gave me the deepest psychological, religious and philosophical insight I had experienced up to that time. Quite possibly this remains the case even today.

Then there was *The Penal Colony* by Franz Kafka (Modern Library). This book includes *The Metamorphosis* and a number of other short fictions which gave me my initial view of fiction's possibilities beyond the realistic or naturalistic. These works remain with me still, even though I have since read many other novels and stories which have dealt with their themes otherwise than realistically. Kafka's relation to the spiritual or numinous has, in my reading, never been surpassed.

Lastly I would list *The Collected Poems of William Butler Yeats* (Macmillan). While Yeats' particular style has not necessarily been the main one I've imitated in apprenticeship years as a poet (or later?), his meticulous crafting of language and his special music were predominant in my own learning of whatever craft I have. I don't think my work much resembles that of Yeats in shape or theme, but my debt is there, nevertheless. For me, still, Yeats is the greatest of the moderns.

TONY HILLERMAN

Author and Vice-President, University of New Mexico. Books include *The Blessing Way, Fly on the Wall, Dance Hall of the Dead, Listening Woman, Great Taos Bank Robbery, Spell of New Mexico* and *New Mexico*. Winner of the Edgar Allen Poe award, 1974, from the Mystery Writers of America, and other national awards.

After some head scratching I'd start with the North translation of *Plutarch's Lives of Famous and Illustrious Men of Greece and Rome*, which I read and re-read when I was 13 and 14, having found them in portions of a library left behind when the Benedictines moved St. Benedict's College from Sacred Heart to Shawnee, Oklahoma. Since there was no library anywhere near our farm, our only access to books was these remnants left behind or by mail-order through the state library. Plutarch, once and for all, turned me on to the magic of the world of books.

181

Then there was *The Will of the Tribe* by Arthur Upfield. Upfield's mysteries set in the Australian outback among the Aborigines formed the germ from which my own effort at Navajo-based mysteries sprang.

The Second Tree From the Corner by E. B. White (Harper, 1935) taught me and re-taught me how absolutely great very simple writing can be. He is the very best there is.

VIDA HOLLIS

Librarian, Northern Regional State Library, Cimarron, New Mexico.

As a child I was particularly fond of *Secret Garden* by Frances Burnett (Lippincott, 1949). I once recommended it to a little library patron, and when she brought it back she said, "Oh, Mrs. Hollis, that was such a good book!" I told Becka that it was my very favorite book when I was a little girl. She said, "Is it *that* old?"

As an adult, I have chosen two historical fiction books that deal with women in the early days of our country. Both seem to fit my philosophy, elicit my sympathy and give me great understanding of both these women's lives and my own. I feel a real tie with both leading characters. These two books are *Tall Woman* by Wilma Dykeman (Holt, 1962) and *Angle of Repose* by Wallace Stegner (Doubleday, 1971).

 182

GARY HOUSE

Librarian, Albuquerque Technical-Vocational Institute.

I will attempt to answer your challenge to identify three books that had the greatest impact on my life. These would begin with *The Secret Garden* by Frances H. Burnett (Lippincott). A wonderful teacher I had in the third grade, Alice Wolf, read this book to us, and that experience opened the doors of mystery, wonder and curiosity. Books came to life; they were more than paper and pictures. There was a light and life locked in the printed words.

Reading *Travels With Charlie* by John Steinbeck while I was a senior at New Mexico Military Institute opened up a vision of what life could be. It gave me balance at a time of dramatic changes both personal and worldwide in the mid-1960s.

Opal by Opal Whitely, arranged and adapted by Jane Boulton (Macmillan, 1976), showed that life is precious, that there is a quality of simplicity, hope and insight in this biography by a six-year-old which carried me to a deeper sense of love.

GENEVIEVE JANSSEN

Longtime bookseller and bibliophile from Taos.

Although books have meant a great deal to me ever since childhood, I can recall only one that had a lasting impact on my life. That was *This Believing World* by Lewis Browne. Macmillan is the present publisher and they list it as World Publication, 1944. But I read it in the 1930s. This book changed my ideas about many things, especially religion. But most importantly it made me realize that I didn't have to accept points of view and attitudes of people I had considered to be authorities. I could do my own thinking and make up my own mind.

DAVID MARCUS JOHNSON

Professor of English, University of New Mexico. Editor of the *San Marcos Review*. Books of poetry include *Pilgrim Country* (1976) and *Indian Rio Grande* (1977). Anthologized in *Voices From the Rio Grande* (1976) and *Southwest: A Contemporary Anthology* (1977).

The first would be Andre Malraux's *Man's Fate* (Random House, 1934). Malraux, in both his life and writings, combined politics and art. *Man's Fate* is about human values, the underbelly of revolution, and life in China during the 1920s. Through his characters Malraux de-

184

scribes the difference between lives committed to social change and lives preoccupied with self-gratification. This remains a modern dilemma: should I try to change anything out in the world, or should I retreat to tending my own garden? Malraux's novel creates a dramatic arena for these ultimate questions.

The second would be C. G. Jung's *Modern Man in Search of a Soul* (Harcourt Brace, 1933). This and other books by Jung opened up the inner world of the psyche for me; the world of symbols and archetypes. Jung showed me how our Western preoccupation with analytical reason and technology had overloaded the masculine side of the psyche, and how we needed to balance it with the feminine—intuition, imagination, spirit, art. Jung showed me the importance of dreams, myth and poetry.

Report to Greco by Nikos Kazantzakis (Simon and Schuster, 1965) records Kazantzakis' spiritual odyssey: Crete, Greece and Italy; Marx, Jesus, Saint Francis, Nietzsche and finally Zorba. Kazantzakis is pulled in various directions as he follows various paths—and in this he represents to me the modern pilgrim and the ongoing dialogue between body and soul.

185

JAMES RALPH JOHNSON

Santa Fe author with over 50 books to his credit, including *Animals and Their Food*, *Zoos of Today*, *Photography for Young People*, *Southern Swamps of America*, *Everglades Adventure*, *Animal Paradise*, *Moses' Band of Chimpanzees*, *Ringtail* and *Anyone Can Live Off the Land*.

The first is *Treasure Island* by Robert Louis Stevenson, an exciting adventure for young people which encourages achievement. The next is *First With the Most* by Henry Forrest (Bobbs-Merrill), a biography of a Confederate leader without equal. Finally, I will name *How I Made $2,000,000 in the Stock Market* by Nicholas Darvis (Heineman, Ltd., Toronto). This is a no-nonsense approach to security investing which provides any person solid results.

TEDDY KELLER

Albuquerque author and Past President of the Western Writers of America. Author of *The Fifty-Niners: A Denver Diary*, *Search for the Hidden Places* and *The Best of Adam*. Screenplays include *A Time to Cry*, *The Smugglers*, *Executive Wives* and *The Shagwood Secret*. Winner of awards for juvenile fiction and short stories.

L. Frank Baum and the *Wizard of Oz* first captured and released the imagination of one small boy, at the same time revealing the joys of the world of books. I can remember walking clear across town to the library and returning with a stack of books, each of them almost as big as I was, and reading them two-a-day.

Richard Halliburton's *The Royal Road to Romance* is the book that first stirred a spirit of adventure and excitement, that sparked curiosity about the world and its people, that forever awakened an attitude of rebellion.

The Oregon Trail by Francis Parkman remains an epic of Western exploration. This book led to a deep and abiding fascination in my own geographical heritage, which led to my first fiction sales, which led to. . . ???

BRUCE KING

Governor of New Mexico. Lifetime rancher.

When I was growing up in Stanley, New Mexico, I enjoyed reading *The Bobbsey Twins* by Laura Lee Hope.

Two books which I have enjoyed as an adult are *Will Rogers* by Donald Day and the autobiography of Harry S. Truman. I enjoy reading about famous individuals and history. I think reading is a good way to relax and learn something at the same time.

Please accept my congratulations on the

187

occasion of the 10th anniversary of the New Mexico Book League.

CLIFFORD E. LANGE

Former State Librarian of New Mexico.

The problem of trying to decide what three books had greatest impact on me has been a difficult one. I have come up with one: *Smoke Screen: Tobacco and the Public Welfare* by Maurine Newberger (Prentice-Hall, 1963). I read and then wrote a review of this book for the Eau Claire, Wisconsin, newspaper in which I had a regular book review column. What this book did was to convince me of the idiocy of smoking. At that time I was about a two-pack-a-day smoker. The night I finished writing the review I made the decision never to smoke again, and I haven't. I am sure other books have had an impact on my life, but I can think of none that compared to Mrs. Newberger's

---

BETTY LLOYD

Librarian of Arthur Johnson Memorial Library, Raton.

House Made of Dawn by Scott Momaday (Harper, 1968) made me realize what a great transition the Indian people are experiencing,

 188

especially the young men returning from war. I found this to be the saddest book I had ever read, but one that had to be written. I shall never forget its grace and veracity as it dealt with a major social problem of our day.

As a librarian, I use *New Mexico: A History of Four Centuries* by Warren A. Beck (U. of Oklahoma Press, 1962) for quick answers to historical reference questions. I can depend on its authenticity and I find the format one of the best on the subject. I often read sections at home merely to refresh my memory of New Mexico's fabulous history.

Whenever I need reassurance I read *The Prophet* by Kahlil Gibran (Knopf, 1923). Gibran says everything I know to be true in an exquisitely beautiful way. I feel this should be required reading for any serious student of life.

MANUEL LUJAN, JR.

United States Congressman, 1st District of New Mexico.

There is only one book which I could name that has had impact on my life. *The Art of Worldly Wisdom* by Otto Eisenschiml, which is three hundred precepts for success, based on the original work of Baltasar Gracian, has been of importance to me. It was published by Duell, Sloan and Pearce in 1947. The insight into

189

everyday life as found in this book has been of great help to me throughout my life.

JENE LYON

Publisher and founder of The Lightning Tree, Santa Fe. Printer of this book.

At about age ten I read a collection of the work of Percy Bysshe Shelley. A world where civilized man can unabashedly express the sentiments and sensibilities of our culture through literature was suddenly and explosively revealed. Shelley's voice is not very prominent now, and I haven't read him for many years, but the memory of that first revelation lingers.

A book little read these days, *The Idea of Progress* by James M. Bury, was the first clue that I had that man's history is short; that many of the cherished ideologies of western society were recent inventions and not as old as the race.

About ten years ago the Club of Rome published *The Limits to Growth*. Ostensibly it is about the natural resources of the planet. But mostly, and in between the lines, it is about the genus *homo sapiens*. No book I have read in the last thirty years has struck me with such force. I think it may be the summary and the schedule of man's impending fate; just possibly it may be

 190

the battle cry for his future. But I will probably not live to see that battle.

JOHN D. McKEE

Author of *Two Legs to Stand On* (1955), *Spanish Times and Boom Times* (1972), *Life and Death of a Frontier Fort* (1973) and *Socorro Photographer: Joseph Edward Smith* (1974), most of which had co-authors. Professor at New Mexico Institute of Mining and Technology, Socorro.

I suppose the greatest discovery in my young life were the essays of Emerson, followed somewhat later by the philosophical works of William James.

These writers came to me just in time to reinforce the conviction then growing in me that a person makes his own life, and that the shaping of the person and the society and environment in which he lives is a mutual act.

Much later, I came upon Aeschylus, most recently in the *Oresteia,* as translated by Robert Fagles and published by Bantam. Aeschylus reaffirmed the idea that a person cannot grow unless he continually tests himself against resistance. Indeed, he puts it more strongly: the gods force man to learn through pain. And what man can learn through the *Oresteia* is the growth of the idea of justice and the notion that the Furies are still there, ever ready to bring

191

mankind back to darkness and to retribution, that we are forever creating the good society, and that if we ever let up, the jungle will close in again.

THOMAS J. McLAUGHLIN

Book salesman and founder of Combined Book Exhibit for libraries.

On reflection, the first would have to be *The Royal Road to Romance* by Richard Halliburton (Bobbs-Merrill, 1925). This book excited me out of my secure "position" to my first real step west of the Hudson River where I went "on the bum" and incidentally experienced my first contact with New Mexico in 1928.

Parnassus on Wheels by Christopher Morley (Doubleday, Page, 1917) was a magnet to the tour I made in my original bookmobile. Originally sponsored by Wilson Co., Bowker Co., American Library Association, National Association of Book Publishers, the American Booksellers Association, and later on my own, I traveled 48 states for 5 years and covered 83,000 miles, visiting thousands of libraries, booksellers and colleges. It was from this experience that I founded The Combined Book Exhibit in 1933.

The third book is tougher, but it's probably *Babbitt* by Sinclair Lewis (Harcourt, Brace,

 192

1922). This book gave me values different from those of my upbringing, and in bromide form to be sure, but they have endured.

JAMES MAFCHIR
Director of the Museum of New Mexico Press, Santa Fe.

The first would be *The Razor's Edge* by William Somerset Maugham. I was in my teens in 1960, stationed at Fort Sill, Oklahoma. Because I was too young to hang out at the beer joints in Lawton, I began to read. What an adventure story! A spiritual quest, leading all the way to a guru in India. This work was a 1930 precursor of the hip movement of the 1960s. I vowed to duplicate that romantic quest as soon as I could.

Then there was *Dharma Bums* by Jack Kerouac. Five years after Lawton, I graduated and had saved up enough money for a round-the-world motorcycle trip. I picked up this book at a London newsstand and stashed it away in my panniers. A month later, recovering from a motorcycle accident in France, I finally had a chance to read the book. Oh how I related to those 1950s beatniks. I had already had many similar experiences during my travels. Rather than abandon my trip, I decided to follow the example of the hero and began to hitchhike.

I did not make it to India as I had vowed, but I hitched throughout North Africa, Europe and the Middle East.

My final choice would be *The Jews* by Howard Fast. Not being religious, I nonetheless have an interest in my roots. I found this paperback in a Santa Fe bookstore several years ago, and it kindled an interest which has led me to many other books on the subject.

EDWIN L. MECHEM

Former Governor of New Mexico. Currently a Federal Judge, United States District Court, District of New Mexico.

I am embarrassed. I have read so darned many books and other similar items over a period of years that I could not begin to pick out three or even a dozen. There are many that I go back to for a variety of reasons. Some that I have to read that make an impact on my occupation and others for pure pleasure. But, thank you for the opportunity at least of casting a ballot.

MARK MEDOFF

Playwrite, whose play *Children of a Lesser God*, received several Tony awards after appearing on Broadway, 1980. Professor at New Mexico State University, Las Cruces.

194

The three books that have had the greatest impact on my life are *Wuthering Heights* by Emily Bronte, the collected novels of William Faulkner and *Catch-22* by Joseph Heller.

The reasons for these three choices are really the same: what I learned about technique, what I learned about the human condition and what I learned about writing sympathetically about characters with whom it is often difficult to sympathize.

GEN. HUGH MEGLONE MILTON II

Retired Army General, Undersecretary of War under President Eisenhower, and former President of New Mexico Military Institute in Roswell and New Mexico State University in Las Cruces.

I would first list *The Story of Civilization*, a series of eleven volumes by Will and Ariel Durant. The first volume was published in 1954, the last in 1975 by Simon and Schuster. This whole series has been a source of information and inspiration to me. To single out one particular volume is an almost impossible task. However, *The Age of Truth* (1959) stands out as the greatest of the eleven.

Next I'd list *Longfellow's Complete Poetical Work*, Cambridge Edition, published by Riverside Press. In my youth we had to memorize

much poetry and, to me, Longfellow was the peer. *Evangeline* is historical; *Tales of a Wayside Inn*, delightful; *Songs of Hiawatha*, enchanting; *Village Blacksmith*, inspiring; and *When Day is Done*, soothing.

The historical significance of *Great River: The Rio Grande in North American History* by Paul Horgan (Rinehart and Company, 1954) holds especially great interest to the people of the Rio Grande Valley. The format is superb, the English is faultless, the description of people and places puts this book in a niche all its own.

JOHN NICHOLS

Taos author of *The Sterile Cuckoo, The Milagro Beanfield War* and *If Mountains Die*.

I suppose books that had the greatest ideological impact on me were a number of things that I read during the Sixties.

Top of the list would be *Capital* by Karl Marx (Modern Library edition). This book, this philosophy, and all the spinoff writing and action around it, changed the direction of my life, what I hope to accomplish with my own writing, and completely redirected the way I understand the world.

The second powerful work might be *The Rise of American Civilization* by Charles and Mary Beard (MacMillan, 1927). I read it around

1967 or 1968, and completely relearned American history, completely redefined my own roots. I feel it was the first time that I was given a fairly straight and honest history of our nation.

The third book was *The Autobiography of Malcolm X* (Grove Press, 1966). This was a powerful exposition of how working class people are treated and try to survive in our country: it's also an inspiring account of how a person can grow, overcome adversity, and strive not only to understand the conditions of our times, but to develop the knowledge to guide their own personal, and greater historical, destiny.

THELMA NORD

Lifetime educator and librarian, Raton, New Mexico.

The books I have read over and over through the years are mostly poetry. The four that have been most important to me are: Palgrave's *The Golden Treasury: The Book of Living Verse* edited by Louis Untermeyer (Harcourt, Brace, 1932); *The Questing Spirit* edited by Halford Luccock (Coward-McCann, 1947); Fitzgerald's *The Rubaiyat of Omar Khayyam*, various editions; and *The Little Treasury of American Poetry*, Oscar Williams, editor.

T. M. PEARCE

Albuquerque author of *Lane of the Llano* (1936), *Southwest Heritage* (1938), *New Mexico Place Names* (1965), *Mary Austin* (1965), *Oliver La-Farge* (1972), *Stories of the Spanish Southwest* (1973) and many articles.

The three books that, I believe right now, have made the greatest impact on my life begin with Samuel Langhorne Clemens' (Mark Twain) *Adventures of Huckleberry Finn* (Harper, 1884). This is not just a good story with an improbable plot, but it makes the riverboat people along the Mississippi come to life and traces the account of slavery in a believable way.

Second is Walt Whitman's *Leaves of Grass* first printed privately by the author in 1856. Both the preface and the contents make a statement combining poetry and prose that are noble and still experimental. No one in the American stream of life has made a greater statement about the nature of America.

Finally is John Steinbeck's *The Grapes of Wrath* (Viking, 1939). The life of the Joads, "Okies" so-called, is an education in survival under the pressure of a harsh season called the Dust Bowl when a social system was ill-prepared for economic instability.

LYNN PERRIGO

Author, historian, educator at Highlands University, Las Vegas, New Mexico.

The truth is that I cannot pinpoint any three books which have greatly influenced my character or career. As I look back now, I realize that I have made procreative use of hundreds of books without letting any few of them use me, and more influential in my life have been good people and bad times.

JAMES POWELL

Las Cruces author of *Death Wind*, *Man Made for Trouble*, *Stage to Seven Spings*, among others.

I am most happy you asked what three books made "the greatest impact on my life," rather than what three I consider simply the greatest. This allows me to go back to a very honest time, when I was young, and I don't have to try to be literary.

All three of my choices were read when I was yet in my pre- or early teens, and they start with *Smokey, The Cowhorse* by Will James (Scribner, 1923). James taught me early on that talent does not always have to be schooled, and that stories as good as any, written by a real Westerner, could come from my native West.

The second is *Green Grass of Wyoming* by

199

Mary O'Hara (Lippincott, 1946), a sequel to *My Friend Flicka* and *Thunderhead*. I almost put *Tom Sawyer* by Mark Twain here, but somehow I read Mary O'Hara more times over. These books instilled in me the true meaning of adventure, as known through the written word.

Finally I shall name *Riders of the Purple Sage* by Zane Grey (Harper and Brothers, 1912). I include this book because what good ol' Zane did for me with this one was what all writers should hope to do for someone else: he made me want to write too! I *think* I'd like to thank him for that.

LEE PRIESTLEY

These three books are a strange combination. An obscure and probably badly written animal story, *Beautiful Joe,* drew even more tears than *Black Beauty*. Date, author and publisher have escaped me. Then, *The Yoke* by Elizabeth Miller (A. Wessels Company, 1908) still reads well and started an enduring interest in ancient Egypt. Finally, *Kim* by Rudyard Kipling (Macmillan) introduced me to the genius of that marvelous Englishman.

I wonder if your other respondents were as

surprised as I at the choices they made. But when I thought about it, these three seemed inevitable.

HARVENA RICHTER

Albuquerque author of the novel *The Human Shore* and the award-winning critical work *Virginia Woolf: The Inward Voyage*. Published in many magazines including *The New Yorker*, *Atlantic* and *Saturday Evening Post*. English Professor at the University of New Mexico.

Because my father was Conrad Richter, I suppose that the books which made the greatest impact on me would all have been his own. *The Sea of Grass* and *The Awakening Land* (the trilogy of *The Trees*, *The Fields* and *The Town*, which won the Pulitzer Prize) had very special impact on me. But his autobiographical novel, *The Waters of Kronos*, was my favorite. This was not only because of it being based on family, but because of its mythic and universal content. These books, as I heard them read aloud by my father to my mother and me, were a reality of my young years equal to that of the present time.

My father's books are published by Alfred A. Knopf, and all but *The Waters of Kronos* are in both hardcover and paperback at the present

201

time, with the paperbacks being published by Bantam.

JACK D. RITTENHOUSE

Antiquarian and rare Southwestern book dealer in Albuquerque, retired Business Manager of the University of New Mexico Press. Author of several books, including *The Santa Fe Trail: A Historical Bibliography*. He hand printed over 50 Southwestern Americana titles for his Stagecoach Press and has won over 40 awards for editorial planning and book design.

I won't count the copy of *Little Black Sambo*, given to me for Christmas in 1916, along with a pair of copper-toed boots when I was four. It was my first book, but not until I was nine and was given a copy of Charles Kingsley's *Water Babies* did I feel that I truly owned my own, personal book. That started me toward acquiring books, and ten years later I owned my first "collection," a set of twenty-eight volumes of Robert Louis Stevenson, all in dime store remainder copies.

The next book that brought an impact, little felt at the time, was James Fenimore Cooper's *The Deerslayer*, given to me when I was eleven. My interest in books about America's moving frontier must have started with that tale.

202

And the third was the *Boy Scout Handbook* which I bought myself when I was twelve. It was my first how-to book, and it taught me that there are few problems whose answer cannot be found in some book somewhere.

They were all good books but not the greatest, yet they started ways of thinking, living and working that changed my life in the long run.

JOHN DONALD ROBB

Composer and author, distinguished Professor Emeritus, University of New Mexico in Albuquerque.

My Musical Memories by the Russian composer Rimsky-Korsakov, tells how, under the encouragement of Balakirev and others, he found the courage and desire to abandon his career as a naval officer and adopt that of a teacher and composer of music. This book, together with the encouragement of Nadia Boulanger and others, especially my wife Harriet, gave me the audacity to do a similar thing when I made the shift in 1941 from a career in the law to a career in music.

Secondly I shall name *Les Miserables* by Victor Hugo. Thornton Wilder, in a speech at an Alpha Delta Phi fraternity banquet, once expatiated on the theme that literature was the

203

"orchestration of platitudes" and this book was a good example of the platitude, "Goodness is contagious," a thought which has been much in my mind ever since.

And finally I will name my own book, *Hispanic Folk Music of New Mexico and the Southwest: A Self-Portrait of a People,* because it epitomizes years of joyous collecting and study by me and my inseparable companion, my wife, of the hinterland folk cultures which so enhance the total picture of our country's culture.

DAVID RUSK

Politician and former Mayor of Albuquerque, New Mexico.

The most important books I probably read during my early childhood. These developed my love of reading. I was a real fan of Winnie-the-Pooh, the Freddy-the-Pig series, and many of the children's classics, such as *Treasure Island* and *Swiss Family Robinson*.

However, several formative books during my adult years include *The Death and Life of Great American Cities* by Jane Jacobs, an urbanist's classic which examines how cities *really* work as places where people must live and work as contrasted with architects' drawing board dreams.

 204

Plain Speaking by Merle Miller was published during the depths of Watergate. These reminiscences of Harry Truman restored my faith in what political leaders should and can be.

Tied for third place are *The Greek Way* and *The Echo of Greece,* both by Edith Hamilton. These are incisive analyses of classical Greek civilization and models of clean, clear, elegant expository style.

TOM RUTHERFORD

Senate Majority Whip, New Mexico State Senate. Balloonist.

Sagebrush Lawyer by Arthur Thomas Hannett (Pageant Press, 1964) gave me a wonderful feeling about the human aspects of our state's fairly recent history. *Fear and Loathing on the Campaign Trail '72* by Hunter S. Thompson (Straight Arrow, 1973) gave me a human insight into national political figures and the political "scene."

But my first important adult reading experience was *The Catcher in the Rye* by J. D. Salinger (Little, Brown). It truly opened the window for me to the literary world.

LOUIS E. SAAVEDRA

President, Albuquerque Technical-Vocational Institute.

205

The only books that might qualify in my case were probably anthologies used in public schools, none of which I can even vaguely recall. They had some wonderful things in them —"The Rime of the Ancient Mariner," "The Raven," "Thanatopsis," "Evangeline."

A few college texts provided an insightful look into school administration and supervision of personnel. My teachers were never real big on titles and authors. Sorry.

POLLY SCHAAFSMA

Author and expert on petroglyphs.

In some cases the books that have the greatest *impact* are not necessarily the greatest books one reads. This is especially true of the first, *The Virginian* by Owen Wister, which I read when I was 10. A later rereading bored me, but at 10 it completely changed my life and aspirations, literally overnight, providing me with a vision of the West and the firm determination, which I never lost, to leave confining New England.

The second book is probably *Heart of Darkness* by Joseph Conrad, which I read in the unbearably sheltered environment of college. It profoundly deepened my sense of the complexity of man and his existence. In some odd way it acted as a sort of rudder for me through those four years and pointed in directions which might be pursued later on.

The last book is J. R. R. Tolkien's *Lord of the Rings*. This trilogy would have been significant at *any* time. Like any good myth, it bears continually on and enriches one's life and perceptions. It is a source of infinite learning, so that one is never through with it.

HARRISON SCHMITT

Former astronaut. United States Senator from New Mexico.

Thank you for your thoughtfulness in including me among the New Mexicans you have asked to contribute to your book.

History of the English-Speaking Peoples by Winston S. Churchill opened my mind to the historical and global interrelationships of freedom, its origins and its peoples.

The Book of Marvels by Richard Halliburton revealed the adventure in seeking history and nature. And, finally, the novels of John Steinbeck and the poems of Robert Frost showed clearly to me the art and power of the written word.

PAUL BIGELOW SEARS

Author, naturalist, ecologist, living in Taos.

As I approach the end of my eighth decade,

207

I cannot do justice to the books to which I am probably most in debt. But I can pay my respects to the following: *Fitness of the Environment* by Lowell Henderson; *Science and Christian Tradition* by Thomas Huxley; and *The Immense Journey* by Loren Eiseley. Thank you for the opportunity to speak up.

MARC SIMMONS

Historian and author of 12 books, including *The Lion of the Southwest* (1973), *Witchcraft in the Southwest* (1974), *New Mexico: A History* (1977), *Southwestern Colonial Ironwork* (1980) and *Albuquerque: A Narrative History* (1982).

The three books that have exerted the profoundest influence on my life are all novels, and two of them are westerns. They are Jack Schaefer's *Shane*, Edward Abbey's *The Brave Cowboy* and Ayn Rand's *The Fountainhead*. Each has heroes who are autonomous, inner-directed and highly moral individuals; and all make an effort, in the best romantic tradition, to depict man as he ought to be.

The reigning fashion, naturalism, that pervades contemporary fiction and non-fiction, and which insists on showing in microscopic detail man as he is—in all his seaminess—I find both boring and pointless.

208

JOHN L. SINCLAIR

Author of *In Time of Harvest* (1943, reprinted 1979), *Death in the Claim Shack* (1947), *New Mexico: The Shining Land* (1980), *Cowboy Riding Country* (1982) among others. Winner of the Western Heritage Award and the Golden Spur Award, both in 1978, and honorary life member of the Cowboy Hall of Fame.

Here are the three books that honestly have most inspired my life. The first would be *Walden, Or Life in the Woods* by Henry David Thoreau. My first reading happened in the 1920s. This book introduced me to the way of life I chose for my fifty-seven years in New Mexico —one remote from the hubbub, fiercely independent, comfortably reclusive—the key point in my final decision to become a writer.

The Best Novels and Stories of Eugene Manlove Rhodes (Houghton Mifflin, 1944 ed.) would be my second choice. Reading Gene Rhodes in the *Saturday Evening Post* roped me into the conviction that the "western story" could be written with dignity... I think *Pasó por aquí* is the greatest western story ever written, a strong ingredient in making me into a writer.

My final choice would be *Pumpkin Seed Point* by Frank Waters (Alan Swallow, 1969). Although my introduction to the American Indian happened in the late 1930s, and the association

most strong from 1944 to the present (I live on an Indian reservation today, as I have for the past 12 years), it was in 1969 upon reading *Pumpkin Seed Point* that I saw the Pueblo Indian in a new light. This was a spiritual light, one that I had been involved with for three decades and unaware of the privilege.

JOE SKEEN

Representative to the U.S. Congress from the 2nd District, New Mexico. Rancher and businessman from Picacho.

The three books come to mind very easily. They are *Tularosa* by C. L. Sonnichsen, *The Rediscovery of New Mexico* by Hammond and Rey and *Chesapeake* by James Michener.

These books and others like them have helped me to better understand why America is such a great nation. This understanding, in turn, has helped me in determining the proper course to take in my day-to-day life.

DIANA and JOE STEIN

Rare book dealers specializing in Southwestern and Western materials. Long-time residents of Las Vegas, New Mexico, they have been involved in several historic preservation projects in the area.

My first choice would be Christopher Morley's *Haunted Bookshop* (Lippincott, 1919), the bookman's bible. I read it every year to inspire me in my chosen field. It inspires me all the more as we are now out-of-print book dealers, helping to bring fine literature back into circulation that would otherwise be lost to future generations. Another choice is Austin Tappan Wright's *Islandia* (Rinehart, 1942). This utopian novel has inspired me to help create a better world. Its setting appeals to me particularly since everyone in *Islandia* is educated, reads books, and literature is not only for the upper classes.

Joe's choice is George F. Ruxton's *Life in the Far West* (Harpers, 1849). It stimulated his interest in western exploration of the United States and the Rocky Mountain fur trade, and started his development of an extensive collection of the mountain men and fur trade. This aspect of American history has appealed to the adventurer in him.

RICHARD MARTIN STERN

Santa Fe author of many books, including *Power* (1976), *Snowbound Six* (1977), *The Will* (1977), *Flood* (1979) and *The Tower* (1974), on which the movie "The Towering Inferno" was based.

I suppose I'd have to start with the Norse myths, which I read pre-school in the children's

211

corner of a Berkeley public library. Their effect on me was both positive and negative. Positive, because they led me into a world I've since spent most of my life in; negative, because by comparison what I found in school the first few years wasn't worth attention.

I'd have to include Kipling, and it's a toss-up between *The Jungle Books* and *Kim*. I devoured them early on, too, and the first short story I sold to the *Saturday Evening Post* was a variant of Kipling's novelette, *The Drums of the Fore and Aft*. Obviously Kiplng was fond of his characters, and I've tried to be friends with mine too. Even the bastards need some saving grace.

John Marquand's *Wickford Point* (Little, Brown, 1939) hit home with a bang, and did much to shape my thinking of the business of writing which at the time I was trying hard to enter. The book was filled with parallels I could not ignore. Jim Calder, the narrator, was a Harvard man, as I am. He wrote for the big slicks, as I was trying to do. He had a professional approach to his work, as Marquand did, which I have always tried to emulate. And he had an agent who became my idea of what an agent should be. Years later, 1947, the model for that agent, Carl Brandt, became my agent—and my symptoms of what had been tentatively diagnosed as ulcers promptly disappeared.

 212

GERALD W. THOMAS

President, New Mexico State University in Las
Cruces. Agriculturist.

In Search of History by Theodore White had
a twofold impact on me. First, the vivid description of Mainland China brought back memories of World War II and helped me understand
the creation of two political and geographic
Chinas. Second, the shocking portrayal of fam-
ine in the Chinese province of Honan forcefully
reminded me that my dedication to the conquest
of hunger must be continued.

The limited edition history of New Mexico
State University, *That All May Learn* by Simon
F. Kropp, provided insight into the functions of
the Presidency and the growth and development
of an institution moving toward diversity and
greatness.

I read *The Blue Nile* and *The White Nile*,
both by Alan Moorhead, while studying the
problems of food production and desert encroach-
ment in sub-Saharan Africa. Moorhead forced
me to look into the role of religion and culture,
as they affect economic and political development in the region that now occupies everyone's
attention.

213

JUSTINE THOMAS

Author and retired proprietor of Villagrá Book Shop in Santa Fe.

The books I have selected are those I would choose if I could have only three books to read the rest of my life.

The first is *Apache Gold and Yaqui Silver* by J. Frank Dobie. These tales of adventure and buried treasure in the Southwest fired my imagination as a twelve-year-old and started me on the path of Southwest literature. Next is *Anthony Adverse* by Hervey Allen. To me the appeal of this book is the beautiful use of the English language.

Old Ugly Face by Talbot Mundy (author of *King of the Khyber Rifles*) is my third choice. This is an esoteric and philosophical novel of India and Tibet when the British army was stationed there. Along with high adventure, it shows the Tibetan way to serenity.

CLYDE W. TOMBAUGH

Discoverer of the planet Pluto. Professor Emeritus, New Mexico State University, Las Cruces.

The Pith of Astronomy by Samuel G. Bayne (Harpers, 1896) is my first choice. This was a small, popular book which I obtained at the age of 12, and was my first introduction to astronomy.

214

Second is *Ancient Peoples* by William C. Morey (American Book, 1915). This was my textbook in Ancient History when I was a freshman in high school. The study of the rise and fall of ancient empires gave me a perspective on long intervals of time and civilizations.

Last is *Mars and Its Canals* by Percival Lowell (Macmillan, 1906). This book greatly increased my interest in Mars and led to my lifelong study of the planet. I joined the staff of the Lowell Observatory in 1929, and discovered the ninth planet at Lowell's Observatory in 1930.

DAVID H. TOWNSEND
Former Director, New Mexico State University at Alamogordo.

The Lessons of History, Will and Ariel Durant (Simon & Schuster, 1968) is the distillation of a lifetime dedicated to tracing man's story. Every line is provocative.

Perhaps *The Grapes of Wrath* by John Steinbeck (Viking, 1939) is the greatest tribute to the American spirit ever written. This masterpiece shows one of the most difficult times in our history and how we survived it.

No one should be granted New Mexico citizenship until he has read *The Milagro Beanfield War* by John Nichols. It could happen only in The Land of Enchantment.

FREDERICK TURNER

Author, living in Santa Fe, New Mexico.

The three books which to date have made the biggest impact on my life are:

John Dos Passos' *U. S. A.* I read this trilogy in the Modern Library edition when I was a college sophomore in 1956. It gave me a wholly different view of our history, one that as a snotty Republican kid I'd never known about. It changed forever my thinking about our culture and its true mission.

Herman Melville's *Moby Dick.* I also read this as an undergraduate student, and its magnificent, rolling prose of the underworld of human existence made a permanent impression on me. It rang far truer and deeper than any theology I'd been exposed to, and I thought then that if this is what it meant to be a writer, why, that would be a grand thing to be.

Joseph Campbell's *Hero With a Thousand Faces.* I first encountered this magnificent work in graduate school and have read it many times since. It is the single work on mythology that seems to me equal in language and insights to the mystery and beauty of the myths themselves.

PETER VAN DRESSER

Author of *A Landscape for Humans* and *Home-grown Sundwellings*, resident of Santa Fe, N. M.

216

During the '30s I was strongly impressed by Oswald Spengler's *Decline of the West,* I think because it introduced me to a sweeping and exciting overview of the vast march of civilizations. I do not now subscribe to all his theories, however. I have recently read Toynbee's *A Study of History,* which I think overshadows Spengler's work and is more humane and perceptive.

In the '30s I was also impressed by Lewis Mumford's *Technics and Civilization.* I recently read Mumford's latest work, *The Pentagon of Power,* which seems to me a very important work also.

Santillana's *Hamlets Mill* excited me because it presents a concept of human evolution from early paleolithic times emphasizing man's awareness and spiritual involvement in the entire cosmos around him, which has been with us since the very beginnings and is possibly the basic characteristic of being human.

Have very recently finished Bertrand de Jouvenal's book *On Power,* which seems to me an epitome of the French intelligence: precise, elegant, logically impeccable and delicately humorous.

FRANK WATERS

Nationally acclaimed author, living in Taos.

The following books have been significant

217

and helpful to me. *Grimm's Fairy Tales*. The flyleaf and first 20 pages of my 520 page copy are missing. But an inscription on the inside front cover shows that it was given to my sister Naomi on her 7th birthday, September 19, 1911. I was then nine years old.

The tales opened up for me the natural heritage of childhood—the invisible spirits and forces of nature, a world of good and wicked fairies, elves, goblins, witches, magic wands, trees and animals who spoke. No such editions exist today. If later thin editions do rarely appear, the tales are revised and expurgated to omit all references to things which self-proclaimed child psychologists deem injurious to a child's "normal" psyche.

The Tibetan Book of the Dead edited and annotated by W. Y. Evans-Wentz (Oxford University Press, 1927). This book, explaining the Tibetan Buddhist doctrine of reincarnation, destroyed for me the limited, rigid, orthodox Christian belief that man lives only one short earthly lifespan, after which he lives for eternity in a blissful Heaven above, or is condemned to eternal tortures in an imagined Hell below.

In this book I found many parallels and similarities to the religious beliefs of our Southwest Indians. *The Tibetan Book of the Dead* also helped me to interpret the paintings comprising the Codex Borgia, the most esoteric of all ancient

 **218**

Aztec codices. The similarity of their meanings is explained in my *Mexico Mystique*.

The Archetypes and the Collective Unconscious, C. G. Jung, published with The Bollingen Foundation by Pantheon Books, 1959. This volume encouraged me to try to interpret my own dreams and to seek in ancient myths the universal truths common to us today. More important perhaps, it emphasized that we must seek the answers to world problems within ourselves, instead of relying upon political and economic measures and war itself.

With the other volumes in Jung's Collected Works, this book has helped me to partially bridge the chasm between modern Western psychology and Eastern metaphysics. A step toward realizing their underlying unity.

VICTOR WESTPHALL

Author, now living in Springer, and builder of the Vietnam Veterans Peace and Brotherhood Chapel near Eagle Nest, New Mexico.

There are a number of reasons why I decided that the Chapel must be built. One is especially important. While I was in the South Pacific during World War II, my wife bought a book for our son David. *Wings for Per* became his favorite childhood possession. His last action before going to Vietnam was to bring the book to his mother and say, "I can't give away this book, it is worth a million other books."

The conclusion of *Wings for Per* reads: "Then I will fly up into the clear, washed air of spring and soar over the eagle's nest and over my home under the crag. Mother will stand in front of the house and clasp her hands in wonder. She will say: 'Look, Per has wings.'"

My second book is my own *What Are They Doing to My World* (Consolidated Publ., Cranbury, N. J., 1980), dealing with 21 specific concerns that confront America. Preparing it consumed a large part of my life for more than a decade.

My third is Stanton Coblentz' *From Arrow to Atom Bomb,* a psychological study of why men fight. Without a solution to the scourge of war, all other facets of man's relationship to his kind and his environment are purely academic.

NORMAN ZOLLINGER

Author of *Riders to Cibola* and *Corey Lane*, officer of the Rio Grande Writers Association and the New Mexico Book League, and proprietor of the Little Professor Book Center in Albuquerque.

A good friend once said to me, "One of your principal troubles in life, Norman, is that your philosophy consists almost entirely of the last book you read." I suppose the only sensible way to make the nominations is to assign them to different times of my life.

When I was very young I wallowed in *King Arthur for Boys*. It seems no longer to be in print by that title, and is definitely not the great old *Boy's King Arthur* which still is. At any rate, this oldest of great legends of our language so stimulated my imagination that I'm afraid I became an insufferable bore to every other kid in our Chicago suburb neighborhood.

In my third year in high school I discovered Ernest Hemingway, particularly *A Farewell to Arms*. No doubt about it, *that* book was the one which convinced me that I would someday write. No one wrote about men at war better than Hemingway did. I honestly think I could teach a one week seminar in the writing of fiction based on the opening paragraph in the chapter where Frederic Henry returns to the front after coming out of the hospital.

During my 25 year hiatus from writing I read and reread a long ton of Joseph Conrad. I could nominate almost a dozen works in the Conrad canon, but after some thought I must opt for *Nostromo*. Conrad's dynamism in describing scenes, as evidenced particularly in the opening chapter, has had a heavy influence in my own work; and while I try very hard not to be imitative, I must acknowledge the deep debt I owe to the writer I consider to be (with the possible exception of Hemingway, of course) *the* master stylist of the English language.

There they are. I make no brief that these are unalloyed *great* books. They're mine.

IN CELEBRATION OF THE BOOK:

Literary New Mexico

This book is set in Caslon, a type face designed by William Caslon (1692-1766), one of the earliest of a long series of distinguished English type founders. Although at one period his type designs were considered old-fashioned and fell into disuse, their clarity and beauty have been discovered by modern designers. As Douglas McMurtrie writes, "In Caslon we have the product of a master designer who made drawing the servant of readability rather than its master."

Our modern cutting of Caslon was specially cast for this book by American Type Founders, Elmira, N. J., and supplied by Heidelberg West, Albuquerque. It was hand-set by Dick Fleming and Jene Lyon in the shop of The Lightning Tree, and printed on a Style B Kelly Automatic Press, ca. 1920.

Other hand produced materials for this book are the marbled end papers, executed by Pamela Smith of Santa Fe, and the 100% rag paper interleaves handmade by Kathy Gurwell in her Santa Fe shop. The rendering of the Spud Johnson Kelsey Press, used as a blind stamping on the cover, was by Madge Fisher Harrah, Albuquerque.

Text paper is 70 lb. Warren's Olde Style Wove, supplied through Dixon Paper Co. in Albuquerque.

The fleurons used in the folios were found among the printing effects of the late Spud Johnson, writer and printer, of Taos. Engravings of these, and other illustrations, by Sunset Color Graphics, Inc., El Paso.

Binding under the supervision of Michael Roswell, Roswell Bookbinding, Phoenix. The binders cloth is Centennial, Kennett and Arrestox from Joanna Western Mills. Text ink made by Gans Ink & Supply Co., Salt Lake City.

This book was designed and printed by Jene Lyon at The Lightning Tree in Santa Fe County, during the years 1981-82. In Celebration of the Book was co-published by The New Mexico Book League & The Lightning Tree
—Jene Lyon, Publisher.

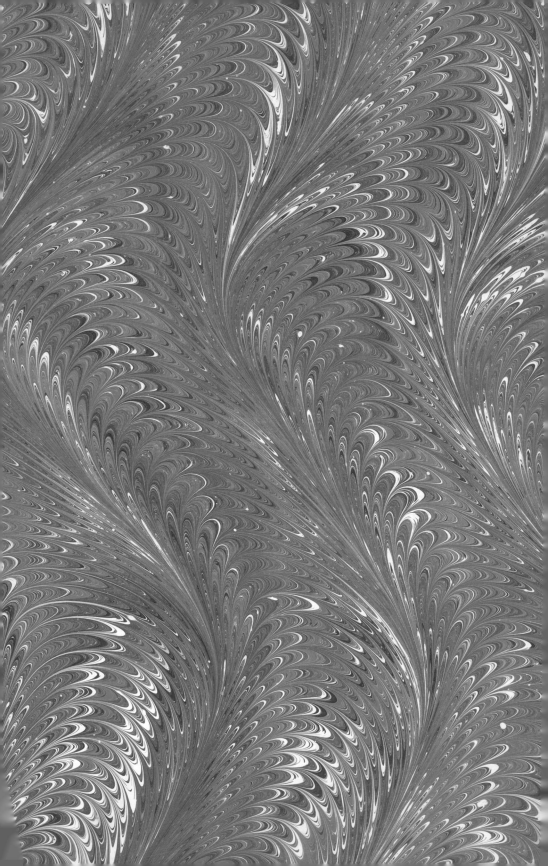